# Need Direction?
# Ask God.

Other books by Dennis Blue

Running the Good Race
Through the Eyes of a Fisherman

# Need Direction?
# Ask God.

Five Biblical Principles for Turbulent Times

Dennis Blue

Mason, Michigan

Need Direction? Ask God. by Dennis Blue

Copyright © 2021 Dennis Blue

Published by Dennis Blue
Mason, Michigan

First Edition July 2021

Paperback ISBN: 978-1-7374070-0-3
eBook ISBN: 978-1-7374070-1-0

Cover image *Silhouette of Mountains* by Simon Berger
https://www.pexels.com/photo/silhouette-of-mountains-1323550/

*To my dear wife Dorothy.*
*Though memories fade,*
*our love endures forever.*

*Whether you turn to the right or to the left, your ears will hear a voice behind you, saying, "This is the way; walk in it."*
*Isaiah 30:21*

# CONTENTS

# PREFACE

I had just returned from walking my yellow Lab, Daisy, and was sipping a hot cup of morning coffee—my favorite time of day. In mid-March 2021, the snow was gone, and I could feel the freshness of spring in the air. Dorothy, my wife and best friend, was still sleeping. She sleeps later due to the Alzheimer's disease that has taken away much of her memory these past eighteen months. I miss our discussions about how God has directed our lives.

It has been sixty-four years since I joined Ford in 1957. Following thirty years of service with Ford, fourteen of which were overseas, I retired and started a charter fishing business. Dorothy and I always considered our lives as consisting of a ministry, and after selling my charter boat in 2016, I was wondering, "Could God open a door to a new ministry for Dorothy and me?" Even with her illness, I knew God wanted her involved.

Where had the time gone? Our daughter Luanne was only fifteen months old when we left for Venezuela in May 1968. Our son Dennis was born in Venezuela. Now they were both grown up with their own children.

In 2017 I began writing. I struggled at first. Not being a writer, I had a steep learning curve. In 2018 I wrote and self-published two books—autobiographies about my life at Ford and as a charter captain. It was gratifying to relive many fond memories travelling the world and guiding customers to exotic fishing locations, but there was something missing. My careers had been satisfying, but now I needed a ministry. God laid it on my heart to write a third book, *Need Direction? Ask God,* about the biblical principles that have guided my life.

Woven throughout the fabric of this story are five principles—prayer, purpose, perspective, passion, and patience—and how they influenced my professional life. Each principle is highlighted and strategically placed in the book using an appropriate life experience to demonstrate its wisdom. My prayer is that you will learn to apply these principles to your own life. May God richly bless and keep you.

# CHAPTER 1: PLANE CRASH IN VENEZUELA

*"Brothers and sisters, we do not want you to be uninformed about those who sleep in death, so that you do not grieve like the rest of mankind, who have no hope." 1 Thessalonians 4:13*

*John and Lucille Hacker, 1968.*

I had been with Ford Motor Company since graduating from Michigan State University in 1957 and worked my way to a management position. Dorothy and I were married in August 1963 after a three-month engagement. The love of my life, she is cute, athletic, and strong willed. In 1968, I was offered the opportunity to work in Venezuela. An overseas assignment with Ford would be a valuable experience to further my career, and Dorothy was the perfect partner for our life as expatriates. Our daughter, Luanne, was now two years old, and Dorothy was expecting our second child in July. We were born again Christians, active in our church, and "living the American dream."

My in-laws John and Lucille arrived in Venezuela on February 28, 1969; it was great to see them again. On the drive to our home in Valencia from the airport in Caracas, they brought us up to date on things at home in the US. Ina, our sister-in-law, was doing fine with her pregnancy, and my mom was well. We were on the same route Dorothy and I had taken eight months earlier when Ford transferred us to Valencia. Everything around us had been so strange then. Now the tour guide, I wanted John and Lucille to experience and enjoy their new surroundings as much as Dorothy and I did.

Now in their mid-fifties, John and Lucille had started a coal and ice business twenty years earlier which had become a profitable fuel oil distributorship with over thirty employees. They loved the Lord, and Dorothy and I enjoyed spending time with them.

To make the most of their trip, we visited several local attractions. The picturesque alpine village of Colonial Tovar, founded in 1843 by German immigrants, was in the mountains near Caracas. We also took John and Lucille to the beach in Puerto Cabello and had them sample the local fresh oysters. Dorothy and Lucille loved going to the International Club and watching Luanne swim. On Sunday, we took John and Lucille to the Fellowship Church and introduced them to our friends. They were impressed with the service and by Joe Semester, who gave the sermon that day. After the service, Joe and his wife Nancy invited us and a few other friends over for dinner. We spent the afternoon chatting and acquainting John and Lucille to life in Venezuela. They commented later how fortunate we were to have made so many friends.

Joe, an engineer with Goodyear, was a large man with a big black moustache and a big heart. He, Nancy, and their two daughters

4

were our best friends and helped us settle into the community. Their love and support would be confirmed in the difficult days to come.

As with most expatriate communities, language is a controlling factor. Consequently, most of our friends spoke English. The interdenominational Fellowship Church was the only English language service in Valencia. If you believed in God and spoke English, that was where you went to church. Dorothy and I made a conscious effort to be involved with Spanish-speaking activities and had many Venezuelan friends that enriched our love for the Venezuelan people. As I was required to speak Spanish at work, it was also a great way to learn the local dialect.

John, Joe, and I made a trip in my plane to the Cunivichie River to camp out and fish for two days. It was a typical 90-degree sunny day in *los llanos* (Spanish for the plains). Beyond the riverside, the plains were barren from the lack of rain during the dry season, but it sported green plants and trees near the river. Joe and I had fished the Cunivichie River before, so I knew John would like to be there despite the heat—and, of course, he was coming from the Michigan winter. We caught lots of peacock bass, *pavon* in Spanish, and a few piranhas. One evening, Joe cooked grilled peacock bass, beans, and potatoes over an open fire, and it was delicious! The *llanos* have a distinct beauty in the evening. The setting sun turns the expansive landscape a soft orange like a sunset over a large body of water. The air cools in the evening, and the stark quietness is broken only by the sounds of birds, frogs, and other nocturnal creatures. We talked about our faith and how God had brought us together in this far-away place. I related to John and Joe how one of my favorite parts of the New Testament was Christ selecting fishermen—Peter, Andrew, James, and John—to be his first disciples, how fishing had always been a passion for me, and now I knew why. "Come, follow me," Jesus said, "and I will send you out to fish for people." (Matthew 4:19). My passion for fishing during

5

those early years was preparation for what has grown into a passion for fishing for souls.

John and I had purchased a plane in the US which we sold when I came to Venezuela. He confessed he missed flying together back in Michigan and looked forward to our return from Venezuela next year. I agreed; we had great times flying together. I reminisced about his generosity allowing me the use his plane to take flying lessons. Neither of us had imagined I would obtain my flight instructor and commercial pilot certification, buy a new plane, and start a flying service in my spare time from Ford. I had purchased a plane in Venezuela as soon as I learned enough Spanish to pass the flight test. I had talked to John about becoming a commercial airline pilot or a missionary pilot, but the Lord had closed those doors. Flying home in the cool cabin of the plane, we could see for miles. John commented on the vast undeveloped interior of the country, miles of brown parched land interspersed with ribbons of green delineating the rivers.

At the airport in Valencia, Joe went home in his car, and as we were driving home ourselves, John commented how pleased he was with our new friends, our church, my work at Ford, and, of course, the plane. "You and Dorothy have been richly blessed," John said. I felt so proud hearing this approbation from John. It impressed on me, at age thirty-six, the importance of my role as breadwinner, husband, and father. John was reaffirming that I was fulfilling those roles, and as far as he was concerned, I was fulfilling them well.

It was March 15, 1969, and our time together was almost over. It had been a pleasant visit, and we all had a great time. John and Lucille made plans to come again in the summer to help Dorothy with the new baby. Lucille was loving every minute of being the expectant grandmother.

That night, we went to bed early as their departure time was eight-thirty a.m. from Caracas. Since the airport was an hour and a half away, John, Lucille, Dorothy, Luanne, and I left home at six a.m. to allow time for check-in and goodbyes. About twenty minutes after leaving home, John realized he had forgotten the airplane tickets and was understandably upset. After a brief discussion, we decided we could go back for them and still have time to make the flight. Fortunately, the tickets were exactly where John thought he had left them, and we were soon back on the highway, rushing to the airport. Fortunately, traffic was light on Sunday at that time of the morning. We pulled up in front of the terminal at eight a.m. For a few extra bolivars, I arranged for an airline agent to handle the luggage, and we rushed John and Lucille through check in. They were processed and ready to board with fifteen minutes to spare. I remember commenting how fortunate we were to have made it back on time. There was little time for goodbyes, so we hugged and waved goodbye as they disappeared down the boarding ramp. It was Sunday, March 16, 1969; we would never see them again.

During the drive home, Dorothy and I talked about how nice it had been to spend time with her parents and how we looked forward to their return. We were back home by eleven a.m. and planned to spend the day relaxing after a busy two weeks, but just after lunch, the phone rang. It was Joe Semester asking if John and Lucille had left as planned that morning. When I replied that they had, he hesitated and asked me if I had heard of the Viasa plane crash in Maracaibo. I said no but not to worry as they had a direct flight from Caracas to Miami. Joe hesitated again and asked if I was sure since a friend of his had a single side band radio and heard that the Viasa flight that crashed in Maracaibo was also headed to Miami. I hesitated, my mind racing to recall the hurried events of the morning, and then I told Joe I was sure the tickets showed Caracas to Miami. I had seen John and Lucille board the plane clearly designated for Miami and did not know why the flight would have been diverted to Maracaibo. We talked a few more minutes about how nice it was to have John and Lucille visit, and Joe repeated that he and Nancy had enjoyed meeting them. I told Joe I was going to do some checking, and if he heard anything else to call me. As I put the phone down, I had an uneasy feeling about the crash in Maracaibo and told Dorothy about the phone call. We agreed it must be a mistake but that I should do some checking just to be sure. I could tell she was upset at the possibility.

When I called the Viasa office in Caracas and Maracaibo, I got busy signals. Communication by phone in Venezuela was generally difficult, and news was slow coming. I contacted security at Ford and asked them if they had heard anything about the Viasa plane crash. They confirmed they had heard of the crash, but they had no details to offer me. I explained the circumstances and asked if they could check as I was unable to get through to Caracas or Maracaibo. They said they would let me know if they heard anything. Dorothy and I prayed together that they were not on that flight and would be safe in Miami. We also asked God to give us the strength and understanding to accept whatever the future might hold.

About thirty minutes later—a long, tense half hour of no news—the phone rang. I looked anxiously at Dorothy, took a deep breath, and picked up the phone. It was my boss, Carlos Medina. We had become good friends over the past months, and I could tell by the sound of his voice that something was wrong. He said to me slowly, "I have talked directly to authorities in Maracaibo, and they confirmed the Viasa flight that crashed in Maracaibo was the flight your in-laws were on. The flight from Caracas was diverted to Maracaibo to pick up additional passengers going back to Miami." Having said this, Carlos then expressed his condolences. A numb feeling came over me; I had heard what Carlos had said but I could not react. It was as if he were talking to someone else, so I said nothing while Carlos continued. "I have arranged for you and me to fly to Maracaibo on the company plane early tomorrow," he said and then hung up.

I hesitated for a moment before putting the phone down myself, not sure if I had even said goodbye to Carlos. I turned to

Dorothy who was standing next to me with tears in her eyes, her face in pain, and without saying a word, we embraced. She had been reading my tone of voice and body language, so she already knew what I had to tell her. We hugged and shed a few tears, but we had not fully realized in our hearts what had happened, so there was no sobbing or emotional outbursts. After a few minutes, we began to talk about how blessed we were to have parents who cared and wanted to be part of our lives, about the time together the past two weeks, and about how ironic—now I would say tragic—that we had hurried not to miss the flight that morning. We were both hurting, more than we could ever imagine. Times like this test what you really believe.

"We asked God," Dorothy said, "for strength to accept whatever the future holds. I don't understand right now, but I trust his word." Deep down inside, we hoped they had miraculously survived. The news was scant at best, and the possibility existed that John and Lucille had escaped the disaster, but we knew the odds were against it.

We decided it would be best for me to go to Maracaibo alone and not ask Carlos to include Dorothy in the next day's flight. There was both Luanne to take care of and the fact that Dorothy was six months pregnant and might not do well in the heat of Maracaibo. The emotional and physical stress of the trip—I could not possibly imagine how bad it would be when I set out—could be too much for her and the child she was carrying. It was now time to call Joe to inform him of the bad news.

"Could you and Nancy keep an eye on Dorothy and Luanne for me while I am gone?" I asked. Joe choked up as he offered his condolences and prayers. I knew Dorothy would be in good hands while I was away.

Dorothy and I then set about the sorrowful task of letting family in Michigan and friends both in Michigan and Venezuela know of the plane crash. Ina answered the phone. She and Ron had heard of the Maracaibo crash on the news, but were John and Lucille on board?

After she asked, I paused and then broke the silence. "Yes, Ina, John and Lucille were on the flight."

I could hear Ina sob. Michigan seemed so far away just then. Soon, Ron came on the phone. Of course, he was incredulous, but I filled him in on what I knew and told him I planned to travel to Maracaibo the next day. After the call, Dorothy and I hugged again. The day's events did not seem real. It was hard for us to accept that John and Lucille had died.

Dorothy had always been close to her folks. I could not imagine her feeling of loss. I was grieving also since John had become a friend, more like a father, but I know my loss was not the same as hers. She was looking forward to the baby and sharing the joy with her folks. We knew Ron and Ina were also grieving, and it was sad that we could not comfort each other. I prayed that God would keep his hand on all of us in the coming days. We would need his strength.

After a few hours' sleep—it was not an easy night—I met Carlos at the Ford hanger for a seven-a.m. departure to Maracaibo. Joe O'Neill, managing director of Ford Venezuela, was also at the plane. He offered his condolences and the resources of the company for anything we might need in the days to come. It was reassuring to know how much people cared about our well-being. The flight to Maracaibo was about an hour and a half during which time Carlos and I talked about the accident. He had arranged for me to stay in a local hotel and had lined up a driver to take me around as needed. Carlos would stay with me until mid-day and then return to Valencia. I would stay to finalize matters and then alert Carlos to send the company plane to pick me up.

The Grano de Oro Airport was partially closed to commercial traffic, but it was accepting smaller aircraft at the executive terminal. Upon arrival, we were met by a representative from our Ford dealership in Maracaibo and a local government official; both offered condolences and updated us on what was known. The plane, a Boeing DC 9, had taken off from the Grano de Oro Airport but was unable to gain altitude. Then, it hit power lines and a pole which tore off the left engine. The plane crashed in the suburb of La Trinidad, two miles from the end of the runway. On impact, the plane burst into flames and spewed fuel and flames for five blocks around the crash site. Many people on the ground were injured, possibly as many as one thousand, and the hospitals were overflowing. The crash would later be determined to be the worst aviation disaster in the world; eighty-four passengers on board— there were no survivors—and seventy-one residents on the ground were killed. A make-shift morgue was set up in a large storage building near the crash site, but it was impossible to go there due to the confusion and the ongoing efforts of rescue teams bringing bodies in.

The tragedy affected many people both in Venezuela and in the US. Our local contact, a smartly dressed man in his forties, had tears in his eyes as he related the crash. He knew people who lived in La Trinidad and was uncertain of their whereabouts. The man suggested we immediately check with the US Embassy as to the protocol for obtaining death certificates. We were informed that we could not be issued a death certificate unless we identified the bodies of relatives killed in the crash to confirm their deaths. Without a positive identification of a specific corpse, there would be a waiting period of up to five years before a death certificate could be issued. During this time, there could be no final settlement of the estate. Since John and Lucille owned a house in Farmington, Michigan, a mobile home in Northern Michigan, businesses, and sundry vehicles, a five-year waiting period could pose serious maintenance and financial problems.

Due to the number of the US citizens killed in the crash— there were forty-seven US citizens aboard including eight from

Michigan—the embassy was overwhelmed handling the questions from relatives. The one benefit I had was being there in person; most of the US citizens killed in the crash had no one in Venezuela to identify them, so their estates were likely to be caught in a legal limbo. It would be difficult if not impossible for someone other than family or friends to identify the bodies and confirm their deaths.

Due to the extremely hot weather, I had to identify John and Lucille as quickly as possible. I contacted several local authorities with the help of our Ford contacts and was finally able to speak to a gentleman overseeing the morgue. With my driver's translation help, I explained I wanted to identify my relatives as soon as possible so as not to be caught in a legal morass. The rapid decomposition of the remains made the task paramount if we were to meet the legal requirements for obtaining a death certificate. Our contact at the morgue was sympathetic and assured me he would do everything possible to assist me. I was given permission to visit the morgue the next morning, and my driver was given location and entrance instructions. Carlos Medina was hesitant to fly back and leave me alone, but I encouraged him to go as I was in good hands and felt the rest was up to me.

That afternoon, I called Dorothy. She said she had not been alone; Nancy Semester had spent the day with her, and several other friends had stopped by or called to offer condolences and help. She said this had been good and she was doing well under the circumstances. I brought Dorothy up to date on the situation regarding the death certificates. She agreed that I should attempt to identify John and Lucille's remains instead of letting the legal process play out. As we hung up, she said, "I love you," in a way that I had not heard her say before, and I knew exactly how deeply she meant it. I replied just as heartfelt, "I love you, too." Our shared mourning deepened our bond beyond what we had ever known before.

That evening I had dinner at the hotel with one of the executives from Clark Industrial Truck. He was Venezuelan, smartly dressed in a suit and tie and greying around the temples, and he spoke fluent English. He looked and spoke like the consummate executive. His company had lost four US executives in the plane crash, and he was there to help guide the families through the tragedy. As we talked, we got onto the subject of eternity. I told him of my faith in Jesus Christ and my belief there was an opportunity for everyone to spend eternity with him. He said he was not so sure as he knew many people who claimed to be Christians but did not act like Christians. I commented maybe he was looking at the wrong point of reference and should focus on Jesus and his message. If the basis of your belief in Christ is what you see in other people, you will likely be disappointed as we all stumble along the way. I quoted John 3:16 to him, "For God so loved the world that he gave his one and only Son, that whoever believes in him shall not perish but have eternal life." I added, "Focus on Jesus, and he won't disappoint you."

He looked at me intently for what seemed like a long time and then said, "You know, you may be right! It's at times like this you wonder about your eternity."

I told him he should give some serious thought to the matter. He replied he would, and he thanked me for the conversation. I mentioned I was going to the morgue in the morning, and he could join me if he wanted to. He declined this offer and said he did not envy me for having to go through that experience.

I slept somewhat that night and was up early for breakfast. The hotel was crowded with people connected with the plane crash. Most were representatives of companies who had lost employees and press reporters, but there were a few relatives of those who had died in the crash. However, I was the only one headed to the morgue. The morgue was only six miles from the hotel, but due to the traffic, it took almost an hour to drive there. We arrived around eight-thirty,

13

and I was shown the entrance. No one accompanied me or asked for credentials. I am not sure anyone knew who I was or why I was there. The building was large—maybe two hundred by one hundred and fifty feet—and consisted of cement block construction with a high ceiling and open windows. I understood from my driver that the building was used on weekends for festivals with music and dancing and there were vendors selling homemade products like jewelry, clothing, and local art—a sharp contrast to its current use.

Inside, there were disfigured corpses and body parts everywhere. Many were burned so badly that it was impossible to recognize whether they were men or women. The remains that were complete bodies were laid on the poured-concrete floor next to each other face up around the entire building, and the remains that were only body parts were scattered in the center. There were eight to ten other living people in the building—mostly emergency workers sorting through personal belongings and arranging bodies. I started my search moving methodically around the building thinking surely I would be able to recognize something to help me identify John and Lucille. Many bodies were severely burned or disfigured with little hair, clothing, glasses, or jewelry to set them apart. I walked up and down the remains without being successful. After the first couple of hours, I had not been able to recognize anything that might have said John and/or Lucille to me, and I had to take a break and go outside.

It was only when I was away from the carnage that I realized how stressful the morning had been. I think the mind has a way to soften the impact of such tragedy. You see it, but the impact is not felt until later. As I sat resting, my mind drifted back to when my dad passed away in 1963 and the spiritual experience I felt being alone with him in the hospital room. I felt the comfort and assurance that God was present and all would be well. That day in the makeshift morgue was different. Instead of the mountaintop experience of feeling close to God, I was in the valley where the reality, stress, and strain of life was painfully evident, where what

14

you believe is tested beyond what you thought you could bear. I was overwhelmed by the enormity of the tragedy—the hundreds of lives that had been impacted! Yet, I knew John and Lucille were with Jesus and prayed the same for the others who had died in the crash.

And then it hit me! I was there looking for two specific people who I knew and loved very much. What about the other corpses? They had someone who knew and loved them! A compassion for the others that I had never experienced before enveloped me. God is not looking for just those who love him, he is looking for all of mankind to spend eternity with him. For the first time I fully understood John 3:16. Not to diminish my sense of grief and loss, but I cannot imagine multiplying it by hundreds and thousands. How God must grieve the loss of every soul not reconciled to him.

Maracaibo, being at sea level, is noted for its high temperature and humidity. I knew I had to finish my task as soon as possible since further decomposition of the bodies would be rapid. After a half hour devoted to rest and a drink, I headed back inside the morgue, determined to find the bodies I was seeking. Again, I walked up and down the rows of mutilated corpses. By three p.m., my hope of identifying John's and Lucille's remains had faded. I had seen nothing that would remotely suggest I could identify their bodies from the dozens of other bodies. As the day progressed, the smell of decomposition had only gotten worse, so I decided to stop for the day and go back to the hotel.

After a shower and a bite to eat, I felt better, but I had not been able to make any headway into alleviating the legal complication that would ensue if I could not identify John and Lucille. I ran into a few others who had been seeking information about their loved ones, but they had done so in more formal circles at the embassy. No one else I met had been at the morgue. I sat in the hotel lobby watching people hurry about, talking loudly, trying to make sense out of what had happened. Some had tears in their eyes; others were shouting into a phone or at the desk clerk for information. Two days earlier, all these people had had other plans for today, and now they were in Maracaibo! How quickly priorities change. Psalm 90:12, "Teach us to number our days, that we may gain a heart of wisdom." I called Dorothy that night to see how she was doing and to bring her up to date. I did not go into detail about the morgue, about the carnage; I said only that I had not identified her parents.

I was thankful Dorothy had not accompanied me and had been spared that traumatic experience. I was discouraged, and I was not looking forward to returning to the morgue the next day to finish the task. When Dorothy and I talk, we can usually come up with a decision that is sounder than one we might make alone. We decided I would go to the morgue one more time in the morning, and if I had no success in a reasonable time, I would select two bodies to identify as John's and Lucille's and report my "identification" to the proper authorities at the morgue. After our decision, Dorothy reflected that I sounded tired and reminded me to take care of myself. I could not imagine how difficult it was for her—Joe and Nancy could only do so much to alleviate her pain.

On my way to the morgue the following morning, the driver, a small man about fifty with a mustache and dark hair, told me how sorry he was that I had to go through such a bad experience. He did not speak English, but I could feel the empathy in his words. I thanked him for his kindness and gave him a pat on the shoulder. The temperature was already in the eighties, and the forecast promised nineties again. The driver let me off, and I walked through the heat toward the makeshift morgue. Even before I entered the building, the smell of the decomposing flesh began to nauseate me, and once inside, I had to cover my face with a damp cloth to mask the odor. The smell, the heat, and the flies were overwhelming.

I forced myself to search about an hour before I conceded how hopeless it was to investigate any further. I wanted to continue for Dorothy's sake and for the memory of John and Lucille, but I had come to the end of the search. As Dorothy and I had agreed I would do, I identified two bodies and began to walk out. As I was about to leave the building, I hesitated and looked back at the surreal scene, feeling one last lingering need to say goodbye to two people I had loved and would miss. I thanked God for the time we had together and that, as Christians, I knew we were not saying goodbye for good. We would see each other again one day in heaven.

After getting the papers from the morgue for the two bodies I had identified as John and Lucille Hacker, I stopped by the embassy and completed all the documents necessary to have American death certificates issued. I was asked if we wanted the bodies sent to the US for burial. The question caught me by surprise. My first thought was, "Why would we want to send remains of someone we didn't know?" Of course, I kept that thought to myself! The embassy official told me if I did not want the bodies flown to Michigan they would be buried in a mass grave with along the others that had not been identified. Although I had not discussed it with Dorothy, I felt that a local burial was the best decision and advised the embassy personnel to go ahead with burying John and Lucille.

I signed a few forms related to the death certificates and burial, and with papers in hand, I turned to leave the embassy as I heard the staffer loudly say, "NEXT." The lines in the embassy were long, and the lobby was packed with people just like me, confused, tired, and hurting. I telephoned Carlos to ask for the company plane to come for me as soon as possible and was told it would be in Maracaibo by one p.m. for return to Valencia later that day.

I called Dorothy. She was in complete agreement with my decision on the burial. We would call Ron and Ina once I got home and let them know there would be no caskets for the memorial and why.

I thanked everyone at the hotel and at the Ford office who had helped me during my stay and shared my gratitude for their kindness. My driver dropped me off at the executive terminal of the Grano de Oro Airport which was still partially closed due to the accident. This was the same driver who had been my companion and translator for the past three days. Not wanting to offend him but needing to convey my appreciation, I gave him a big hug, placed a few American dollars in his hand and walked away. We departed Maracaibo at two p.m. after a bit of lunch at the airport. It was good to see Captains Baroni and Mora who both offered their condolences. I could tell they shared my grief.

I was the only passenger on the plane heading back to Valencia. The past few days had been overwhelming. I was tired and emotionally drained. It is hard to think clearly when you are grieving. Had God brought us to Venezuela to live this loss? Why us Lord? We have been good Christians, teaching Sunday school, Bible study, singing in the choir, and living a Christian lifestyle. Is God really in control? Was coming to Venezuela a mistake? I accepted Jesus as my personal savoir in 1962 and was baptized shortly thereafter. I stumbled along the way but continually grew in my faith and love of Jesus. For the first time in my Christian life, doubt had emerged. I was reminded of John 16:33b, "In this world you will have trouble. But take heart! I have overcome the world." and Romans 8:28, "And we know that in all things God works for the good of those who love him, who have been called according to his purpose." I focused on the word ALL, not just some things but ALL things. Either God is in control, or he is not. Until now life had been so good—a loving wife and daughter, family, friends, a great job, and pursing my hobbies of flying and fishing—and then it all came crashing down. As I dozed off in the airplane flying high over Venezuela, I did not understand but was at peace with words of Proverbs 3:5–6, "Trust in the Lord with all your heart and lean not on your own understanding; in all your ways submit to him, and he will make your paths straight." I recalled Dorothy's words to me three days earlier when we learned of the crash, "We asked God to give us strength to accept whatever the future holds; I don't understand right now, but I trust his word." I was beginning to understand the full meaning of her words.

John and Lucille are interred at Cemetery Sagrada Corazon de Jesus in Maracaibo at the site of a memorial for those lost on Viasa Flight 742 on March 16, 1969. It was subsequently determined that the cause of the crash was faulty runway sensors, and the plane was overloaded by more than 5,000 pounds. Due to prevailing conditions of high ambient air temperature and the length of the runway, the airplane did not gain sufficient airspeed for flight.

In Valencia once again, it was good to be back home with Dorothy and Luanne. I never felt so blessed. It is true that difficult times draw you closer. We hugged for a long time. I then called Ron and Ina to bring them up to date. I told them of my decision on burying John and Lucille, and they thanked me for not putting them through the experience of having two random bodies at the memorial. We decided to have a memorial service the following week in Michigan. Due to how quickly events had transpired and how far away Dorothy and I were, we agreed Ron and Ina would make all the decisions regarding the memorial back home.

We left for Michigan on March 20. As we boarded the Viasa flight to Miami, we could not help but think of John and Lucille boarding the same flight four days previously. I thought of how fragile life can be. For John at age fifty-four and Lucille at age fifty, their future together, their plans to return for our baby's birth, and their hope of seeing their grandchildren growing up ended in the blink of an eye. Dorothy and I had also seen our future changed. It would be a future without John and Lucille. I would sorely miss John, my flying buddy, and the great times we had together.

The memorial was held March 26, 1969. Calvary United Missionary had been our home church since we were married, and we missed our pastor and friends. Barring the circumstances, it was great to see them all again.

19

After the memorial, we got together with Ron and Ina to grieve and celebrate John and Lucille's lives. We talked about the future and the new babies, how John and Lucille had looked forward to being grandparents again, and how in the blink of an eye, joy turns to sadness and priorities change. It was tough, very tough, but everyone was holding up well under the circumstances. My mom sympathized with us. My dad had passed away the year before Dorothy and I were married, so now she was alone. She was fond of John and Lucille, who had been kind to her and ensured she was always invited to family gatherings.

I was so proud of Dorothy. She was grieving, but she never wavered in her faith or questioned what had happened. It would have been so easy to allow this tragedy to overwhelm us with pity and grief. Guilt had begun to raise its ugly head; had we not moved to Venezuela, John and Lucille would be alive today. Instead, it had drawn us closer together. I knew I had married a strong-willed woman, but I had never imagined how important her strength of personality and convictions would be in this difficult time. The natural inclination is to look for someone or something to blame. We live in a world where bad things happen, but it is how we respond to what happens that matters. We choose to believe Romans 8:38–39, "For I am convinced that neither death nor life, neither angels nor demons, neither the present nor the future, nor any powers, neither height nor depth, nor anything else in all creation, will be able to separate us from the love of God that is in Christ Jesus our Lord." We prayed for the other one hundred and fifty-five souls that were lost and their grieving families.

We considered moving back home and being close to Ron and Ina and my mom. Ford had already offered to do anything to help, so I knew they would support us moving back to the US. We could pick up where we had left off; the house was still there as was the mobile home at Glen Lake. Our church, our friends, our family—everything would be the same. But not really, we could not bring John and Lucille back. In the end, we decided not to return to Michigan before our scheduled time. We believed we were in Venezuela because God wanted us to be there, and we were going to see it through. We did not know the purpose, but it did not take long to find out what God had in store for us. As Paul wrote to Timothy in II Timothy 1:7, "For the Spirit God gave us does not make us timid, but gives us power, love and self-discipline."

# CHAPTER 2: A NEW BEGINNING

*"Being confident of this, that he who began a
good work in you will carry it on to
completion until the day of Christ Jesus."*
Philippians 1:6

*(left to right) Don Bodine, son Mark, Bob
Dunbar, Dennis Blue, and Ron Bodine
in San Juan, Venezuela, 1969.*

We arrived back in Venezuela on April 3. It was good to
return to work and to our new friends. So many people
acknowledged our loss and offered to help. Our dear friends Joe and
Nancy stopped by to see if they could do anything for us, and just
having them around was a big help. We will be forever grateful to
them for the support they gave us during those difficult days and
months.

The Fellowship Church held a memorial for Dorothy's folks. Of course, many of the congregation remembered John and Lucille's visit of only a few weeks earlier. There were tears and joy, and the experience gave our fellowship a new depth to the meaning of being brothers and sisters in Christ.

Settling back into our normal life in which grief would not be so overwhelming took time. There were moments when we found ourselves remembering John and Lucille and tears would come to our eyes. Being back in Venezuela, not expecting to see them each day as we did back home, lessened the impact of their absence. Unfortunately, it would not be that easy for Ron and Ina living only twenty minutes from where John and Lucille had been living. In time, we began to accept what had happened. Our faith was tested to the core, but we had never felt so close to God. Without the assurance that John and Lucille are with our Heavenly Father, I am not sure we could have overcome the grief. Expecting the baby was good for Dorothy as she and her friends were busy preparing for the arrival.

I stayed close to home after the accident to be with Dorothy to support her in her grief. However, the second week after our return to Venezuela, she said to me, "Don't you think it's time for you and Joe to go fishing?" I looked at her, my face turned into a question, and she began to laugh, "I know you have been waiting for me to say that."

"That's my wife," I thought, "always thinking of someone else." I hugged her and said, "I thought you were never going to ask." We both knew we needed time for healing, but we also needed to resume our normal lives and time with friends—and that, too, was healing.

On April 12, Joe and I made a one-day trip to the Cinaruco River. It was the same spot John, Joe, and I fished together during John's visit in March. It was great to be flying again, yet I could not help but think of John and our time together just four weeks ago.

Over the next several years, Joe and I made numerous trips to the interior of the country to fish for peacock bass. We would fly down in my Cherokee 235 for a day or two of camping on the river. As we got to know the area, we would pick a site along the river where we could safely land to try the fishing. Before landing, I would fly close enough over my intended landing strip to look for potential hazards such as logs or ant hills. I could not know who owned the property as there was no sign of habitation for miles around.

Joe and I were always mindful of our surroundings; any kind of injury so far from help could be serious if not fatal. Since Joe was not a pilot, if I were incapacitated and not able to fly, the options for getting help were minimal. I always carried a survival kit in the plane (flares, first aid kit, flashlight, canned food, blankets, water, and a handgun).

Joe and I returned from our one-day fishing trip on Sunday, April 13, in time for church and a board meeting following the service. The Fellowship Church board was developing new practices to improve our church ministry. I volunteered to attend a church service at the International Church in Maracay, about an hour's drive north of Valencia to observe how they conduct their service and report back to the board.

It was Sunday April 20, 1969—a day that would initiate profound changes in our lives—when Dorothy and I attended Sunday morning service at the International Church in Maracay, thirty miles north of Valencia. Maracay had a population of about 600,000 at the time and served as home to the largest air force base in the country. I had no idea how much of an important role this air force base would play in my future. I only knew that I was in Maracay because our church board wanted to see if the International Church's "best practices" could be adopted by our Fellowship Church.

Following the service, I met with Venezuelan businessman Clayton Guzman, a member of the International Church board who was also active in the Christian church. A fluent English speaker, he was smartly dressed and handsome with a touch of grey in his dark hair. In Caracas, where he had his home, he worked as an executive in the insurance industry and was well known and respected by many in the Venezuelan government. During our discussion on church outreach, Amazon missions came up. Clayton was involved with helping New Tribes Mission (NTM) extend its ministry in the remote Amazon Territory. NTM, founded in 1942, is an international evangelical Christian mission dedicated to spreading the good news of Jesus Christ to indigenous peoples by translating the Bible into their languages.

"Be in touch with Jim Bou. He is one of the NTM field directors in Puerto Ayacucho. That is the capital of the Amazon Territory," he said, and then he wrote Jim's name and phone number for me. "Telephone communication with Puerto Ayacucho can be difficult, and it might be better to send a letter if you are not in a hurry."

On the way home that day, Dorothy and I discussed working with New Tribes Mission, and I told her how I felt God had called us to do this. She said she supported me and would do what she could to make this work for us as a couple following the Lord's calling. I responded, "I think this may be why we came to Venezuela; God wanted us here."

After numerous unsuccessful attempts to call Jim, I decided I would fly to Puerto Ayacucho rather than contact Clayton Guzman for help. At this point, Dorothy was almost seven months pregnant, and while I would have loved to have her with me, it did not seem reasonable to put her through such a trip. She agreed. I asked Joe Semester if he would like to accompany me, and he was as delighted to join me as I was to have him with me.

As recorded in my flight log, on May 7, 1969, Joe and I made our first trip to Puerto Ayacucho, a city of approximately 28,000 on the Orinoco River, three hundred and ten miles and two and a half hours flying time south of the municipal airport in Valencia. The area we flew over, known as Los Llanos, consists of miles of undeveloped, sparsely populated land. Tributaries of the Orinoco, many of which Joe and I had fished, fanned out across the plains providing life-giving water during the dry season. In the rainy season, the rivers overflow their banks for miles, making it almost impossible to travel by land. Joe and I had flown over some of the northern reaches of this area before, but we had never come this far south.

The airport in Puerto Ayacucho had sufficient runway length for small turbo jets and was equipped to handle the daily Viasa flights between Puerto Ayacucho and Caracas. I would come to know the airport well as a re-fueling stop on my way to and from the Amazon. Puerto Ayacucho, besides being the capital of the Amazon Territory, was also a river port for barges and various smaller boats to move supplies up the Orinoco River into the Amazon or down river to the Caribbean. Infrastructure to support an urban life was basic: retail produce was limited, drinking water and sanitation were marginal, and electrical power was subject to daily outages.

Joe and I arrived in Puerto Ayacucho at eleven-thirty in the morning. After checking in with airport authorities and having a bite of lunch, I inquired as to the location of the New Tribes Mission headquarters, and the first person we asked gave us directions. Since the office was about three miles from the airport and the sun was rather hot, we took a local taxi—a 1950's vintage Toyota that needed new upholstery—rather than walk. It was a rough ride as the road had no shoulder and numerous potholes. Other traffic we saw on the two-lane asphalt roadway consisted mainly of commercial trucks transporting products to the port for shipment south along the Orinoco River.

Once at the New Tribes Mission headquarters, I knocked on the door of the green stucco building and introduced myself to the man who answered. He was Don Bodin, an American missionary with New Tribes who oversaw administration and supply. Don welcomed us in and introduced us to his wife, Jean, and eight-year-old son, Mark. Then, Joe and I described how we came to be in Venezuela, my contact with Clayton Guzman, and our interest in missions. Don, who also knew Clayton Guzman, explained that Jim Bou lived with the Maquiritare tribe in the remote village of Acanana, two hundred miles from Puerto Ayacucho. Communication with Jim could only be made by mission mail or radio.

Don and Jean were in their mid-thirties and energetic about mission work. Joe and I liked them from the beginning, finding our experiences and their work in Venezuela to be a good mix, and they were obviously pleased to meet us. When Jean asked us to stay for the night, we declined at first, thinking we would be imposing on them, but we relented after Jean insisted.

It seemed we had come at the right time with our offer to contribute to the New Tribes mission. Don told us Missionary Aviation Fellowship (MAF) had provided air support for them during the past several years. Unfortunately, two years earlier, their sole pilot was killed in a crash on the way to one of the mission bases. It took two years for MAF to assign a new plane along with a new pilot. Shortly after arriving, the new pilot came down with malaria and, for the past several months, had been unable to fly. In the absence of the plane, all supplies had to be shipped to the mission bases by canoes and barges. By boat, it took five to seven days to transport goods from Puerto Ayacucho to TamaTama, the main New Tribes Mission base in the Amazon Territory.

We discussed the possibility of using my plane to fill in for the sick pilot, and I was willing to pay for the gas. It was standard procedure for MAF to charge a per-hour cost for their services much like commercial cargo services, which were almost non-existent and therefore not an alternative to MAF. The high cost and risk of

27

maintaining a flying service in the Amazon that made it financially prohibitive for commercial carriers was also what made MAF the only viable means of air transport and explained why it took so long to return to service. Fuel was not always available; maintaining planes in top condition was an extreme challenge in an area where supplies and facilities were at a premium; skilled pilots were hard to find and keep; navigation systems were lacking; the airstrips were dangerously short and experienced occasional mishaps; and the weather was either too hot or too wet. All these factors minimize profit potential. Even with support from numerous Christian organizations, MAF's per-hour cost was double that of a similar operation in a commercial market.

As Don Bodin and I talked about this, I told him I did not want to appear in competition with MAF. I was offering my help for free, and I did not want this to create hard feelings between NTM and MAF. Don did not feel that was a problem as MAF was not sure when it would fly again. In addition, the use of MAF was restricted due to the high cost involved. I would only complement what MAF was doing, and NTM needed help.

That first evening, Jean prepared a delicious dinner of pork and local squash. After the meal, we talked late into the evening. Don wanted to check with the other field directors before finalizing decisions about taking me on. Dorothy and I would also need to discuss the nature and the level of our involvement before committing to anything. We agreed that Don would plan for NTM field directors Paul Dye and Jim Bou to travel to Puerto Ayacucho, and I would return in two weeks to pursue the matter.

On the way back to Valencia, Joe and I were excited about the possibility of helping New Tribes. When I arrived home and told Dorothy of our meeting, she was as excited as Joe and I were. Without saying a word, tears came to our eyes as we realized this was why God wanted us to return to Venezuela. Dorothy and I knew, based on what I had discussed with Don and Paul, that there would be potential risks flying in the Amazon. I admit, at age thirty-six, I still thought I was invincible, but this was not about being foolish or careless. It was about a ministry God had called us to do. As a pilot, I was well prepared with over a thousand hours of flight time. I knew in my heart of hearts that John and Lucille, along with the other saints in heaven, were cheering us on.

Joe was unable to accompany me on my return flight to Puerto Ayacucho, so I made the trip solo. Don Bodin met me at the airport and drove us to the NTM headquarters where I met both Jim Bou and Paul Dye. Jim, an American missionary, was thirty-seven years old and had been with NTM in Venezuela since age twenty. Jim was introduced to Christianity in his teens, and he knew from the day of his conversion that missionary work was his calling. A big man, two hundred and twenty pounds with a dark complexion and blue eyes, Jim Bou was fluent in Spanish and several tribal languages learned from working with natives in Venezuela. Like many other New Tribes missionaries, Jim was trained at the New Tribes Bible Institute in linguistics. Jim told me it had taken him five days by boat to reach Puerto Ayacucho for our meeting. He had just finished a complete translation of the New Testament in the Maquiritare language and was awaiting the final printing of the New Testament Bibles in Caracas. Clayton Guzman was helping with the funding and printing. Jim had never married, and he considered the Maquiritare his family.

Paul Dye was raised on the mission field. His father, Cecil, and Paul's uncle were two of five missionaries that lost their lives in 1943 trying to contact the Ayore tribe in Bolivia. At the time of his father's death, Paul was in Bolivia with his mother and sister. The book *God Planted Five Seeds*, a best seller in Christian bookstores, recounts the efforts of these brave men to contact the Ayore. Paul and his wife Pat, both in their mid-twenties, and their two young children Larry and Lisa were now based in TamaTama and worked with several tribes in the Amazon Territory.

29

After introductions, Paul, Jim, and I talked more about my Christian values and the help I could provide them. I related how Dorothy and I came to be in Venezuela and the tragic death of Dorothy's folks in the plane crash. I was surprised to learn they were aware of the Maracaibo crash; Paul related how, even in the remote regions of the Amazon, news travels by word of mouth. They believed my being in Puerto Ayacucho was an answer to prayer as their work had been extremely difficult since MAF had been unable to fly them or their supplies. We outlined what role I would play and how often I could participate. I told them my schedule would be somewhat limited by the demands of my job at Ford, but we could work around that. There was also the issue of my growing family.

One interest Paul brought up was an aerial survey of the region east of San Juan de Manapiare, one hundred miles southeast of Puerto Ayacucho. Don Bodin's brother Ron and his wife Avis were based there and reported signs of tribal activity not known to the mission. It was agreed we would meet in San Juan in September, after the rainy season, and do an aerial survey of the region. No one anticipated what might lie ahead!

Back in Valencia, word had spread to the Fellowship Church and the Ford office of my trip to Puerto Ayacucho and my intent to work with the missionaries. Much to my surprise, I received support from almost everyone at work and among the expatriate community. I kept my plane at the Ford hanger where I would see Captain Baroni, Carlos Morra, and Señor Serra, the chief mechanic, several times a week. They were enthused about my flying to the Amazon and offered to help in any way they could. Señor Serra commented several times how he double checked everything to keep the plane in perfect flying condition. I was grateful for his attention since, as the death of the MAF pilot demonstrated, there was no room for error when flying down over the jungle.

Dorothy gave birth to our son Dennis on July 5, 1969. We had hoped for an American Fourth of July baby, but we missed our due date by one day! Dennis, however, did not miss being born on an Independence Day—on July 5, 1821, Simon Bolivar had declared independence for Venezuela from Spanish rule.

Joe and Nancy were with me at the medical clinic when Dennis was born. Most expatriate women went to Caracas to have their babies due to the better medical care there. Dorothy, however, was content to stay in Valencia so she could be close to me, Luanne, and our friends. The care and help she got from Nancy, Esther—our Trinidadian maid—and other friends when she got home convinced us it was the right decision. Esther loved little Dennis from the beginning. Later, we would kid Dennis that he thought Esther was his mother since she spent so much time with him.

On July 6, when I called Ron and Ina to let them know of Dennis' birth, Ron had just gotten home from the hospital where Ina had given birth to their son John that morning. Both Ina and the baby were fine. When I told Dorothy the following morning, she was so happy for them and could not wait to see little John. We smiled as we wondered how Lucille would have handled the situation.

Dennis was a Venezuelan citizen by location of birth and a US citizen by parentage. The day we brought him home, we sat for a while with Dorothy holding Dennis. How we wished John and Lucille could be there physically to welcome their new grandson into the world, but spiritually, we knew they were with us.

My mom came for two weeks in September 1969. We really enjoyed having her with us. She was the only parent we had left, and it was a blessing for her to spend time with Luanne and Dennis.

Since Paul Dye and I first discussed doing aerial surveys, I had been anticipating the end of the rainy season. While airstrips at other NTM bases were usable during the rainy season due to higher elevation, the airstrip at San Juan de Manapiare was near sea level and prone to flooding from April through August. I could not make my first foray into the Amazon until the rains stopped. On September 14, 1969, the day after Mom returned to Michigan, I flew to Puerto Ayacucho to pick up Paul Dye and then on to San Juan de Manapiare to begin the aerial surveys of the region.

Due to the uncharted nature of the Amazon Basin and the increased security concerns about Columbian guerillas, the Venezuelan government restricted planes flying in areas that were not registered and accounted for. With the help of my good friend Captain Baroni, who had connections with the Venezuela authorities, I obtained my permit to fly in the Amazon Territory of Venezuela. Government regulations required I check in, either by radio or in person, with the airport in Puerto Ayacucho when entering or leaving the Amazon Territory. I could not have imagined it just a few months earlier. "Why me?" I thought, but that would be revealed in the days to come.

Other tribes reported sighting human activity in the area, but we had no information as to location or tribe. Only God knew what lay ahead. Would we find evidence of an unknown tribe and, if so, could contact be made and at what cost? Ron and Avis Bodin, who had grown up in the mission field, worked with the Piaroa tribe in San Juan, one hundred miles southeast of Puerto Ayacucho on the Ventuari River. The town had approximately three hundred and fifty residents, mostly Piaroa natives, and was recognized as a municipality by the State of Amazonas. Electricity was provided by two large generators perpetually in need of repair; power outages were a daily occurrence. The airport, one of the largest in the region, had a grassy 1,200-foot airstrip which was still a little soft from the rainy season.

After landing, Paul and I were met by Ron Bodin and a couple of Piaroans who helped us carry our supplies to the mission house a half mile away. The narrow dirt road into town was still muddy from the rain, and a few dogs and chickens scattered about to welcome our arrival. Ron told us the town seldom flooded since its elevation was about fifty feet higher than the airport. We spent the evening with Ron and Avis Bodin, and Tom and Lila Blinco joined us for dinner. Tom and Lila were from England and had adopted a native Yanomama baby girl who had been abandoned since her birth mother could not take care of her—a harsh reality of life in the jungle.

Everyone was excited about the survey, and we sat around after dinner making plans and going over a map I had made of the area. Using this map as a guide, each time I flew in the Amazon, I noted villages, rivers, and mountain ranges not already on my map. I also marked each flight path on my map using time, compass heading, speed, and landmarks for accuracy. Using the same principles, I could accurately mark the locations of villages on my map each time we left San Juan.

The morning of September 15 was calm and clear, perfect for flying. About thirty minutes east of San Juan, we spotted several huts that Ron recognized as Piaroa. He could tell which tribe built the huts by their construction. Twenty minutes later, on the Iguana River, a tributary of the Asita River, we saw more huts almost hidden by the dense jungle foliage. Ron did not recognize the construction of these huts and felt this was our objective. After several more passes overhead taking coordinates and gathering information on what we saw on the ground, we flew back to San Juan where there was much excitement among the missionary families and the Piaroan believers. That evening, Ron and Paul began planning to make contact the following week. The terrain was hilly and dense, so the initial contact would involve a difficult land trip requiring three or four days by boat and foot. It was good the rivers were still a little high from the wet season as this would allow easier access by canoe. The sooner they initiated contact the better, as tribes sometimes move to other locations. I had not planned on going due to my work schedule. Making a trip like this in the jungle required survival and language expertise which I did not have, and I would have been more of a burden than a help. Although nothing was said, I could not help but wonder what Paul and Ron's wives and families were thinking. Fifty-three years earlier, their fathers had embarked on a similar trip and had never returned. The next morning, before I returned to Valencia, Ron, Paul, and I flew over the same area to confirm the location. This time we saw smoke and freshly cut trees on the ground. I planned to return the following week to see if contact had been made.

The next week flew by at work, but I could not stop thinking of Paul Dye and Ron Bodin and praying they would safely accomplish their mission. Anxious for an update, I took Luanne, who was only two and a half, with me and flew to San Juan de Manapiare on September 29. Luanne had asked to go to San Juan with me, and as I had to return the next day, I decided this would be a good opportunity for her to meet everyone. She enjoyed playing with the Blinco children.

Upon arrival, I learned Paul and Ron had left San Juan on September 23 and had been in contact with San Juan each day by mission radio. Contact with the unknown tribe had been made, all had gone well, and they were on their way home. I thanked the Lord for their success and prayed for their safe trip back. Paul and Ron did not arrive in San Juan until after I had returned to Valencia, so I had to wait until I saw Paul several weeks later to get a first-hand account of their introduction to the new tribe, the Yuwana.

After a month, I was growing anxious for an update. In November, Jim Bou wrote to me that he and Ron Bodin had gone to stay with the Yuwanans for a month to begin language study. Jim later told me the language was extremely difficult, and it would take time to develop a written language so the New Testament could be made available to them. Over the next year, as time permitted and the need arose, I made flights for NTM, but I continued to be busy—enjoyably—at work.

In January 1971, I received a letter from Tom and Lila Blinco. They had moved in with the Yuwana for a year but left the past November to replenish supplies in TamaTama. When they returned, the Yuwana had moved. Based on the growth of vegetation and spider webs on the huts, they had been gone several weeks. It is not unusual for tribes to move in search of food or in fear of another tribe, and if or when they would return was unknown. The Blincos decided to stay and complete their new house and to work on the Yuwana language using the tape recordings and notes of their previous visit. I admired Tom and Lila's dedication. The difficulty of living in the jungle alone with small children is hard to comprehend. Even with supplies, sustaining life in the damp, insect-infested environment with limited food, water, medical supplies, electricity, and communication with the outside world is not for the faint of heart. Malaria, dysentery, or hepatitis is only an infection away. I prayed for God to protect and sustain the Blinco family.

The last I heard when I left Venezuela in 1972 was the Yuwana had not returned, and Tom and Lila eventually had to leave the work due to health reasons. During the ensuing years, I heard nothing more of the work with the Yuwana. It was not until I received an email from Larry Dye, Paul's son, on October 30, 2016, that I learned the outcome. A quote from Larry's email to me reads as follows,

> "Today is Dad's birthday. He is seventy-six years old. Yes, I remember your name mentioned many times down through the years! You played a big part in the start of what took many years to accomplish in planting indigenous tribal churches among the Yuwana and the upper Orinoco tribal groups. God gave me the privilege to fly in Venezuela for fifteen years. I also had the privilege of being there to see the birth of the Yuwana church, which because of many unforeseen plots from Satan, our enemy, because of a language that was considered one of the hardest to break down, and because many missionary families had come and gone, it took over twenty-two

years before the gospel was presented in their own language."

Tears welled up in my eyes as I thought of the many dedicated people who were involved in bringing the Bible to the Yuwana.

# CHAPTER 3: AN AIRSTRIP IN THE AMAZON

*"What is impossible with man*
*is possible with God." Luke 18:27*

*Loading a Ford tractor at Las Esmeraldas, 1970.*

We went home to Michigan for Christmas in 1969. Ron and Ina hosted Christmas at their new house in Canton, Michigan. Dorothy and Ina could not wait to introduce Dennis and John to each other. Several of Dorothy's aunts, uncles, nieces and nephews and my mom were in attendance—there were twenty of us. We had a great time seeing everyone again, but there were a few moments of sadness as we recalled John and Lucille who had been with us the previous Christmas.

We had decided to sell John and Lucille's house, and the broker arranged a closing while we were home during the holidays. The day before we closed with the new owners, we stopped by the house. It looked brand new inside, ready to welcome its new owners. As we strolled through the house, we had a moment of seller's remorse. "Maybe we should have kept the house!" we suggested to each other. We shared how when I first met Dorothy's father he realized he and I had met several years before. At dinner he had been able to pull out my business card from his wallet to prove it. How proud and excited they were of their two granddaughters, Luanne and Rhonda, born three days apart. Those had been good times, but then reality set in. John and Lucille were gone. No matter how hard we wished otherwise, this house would never be the same welcoming home we had known. As I closed the front door behind us one last time, we knew we were closing the door on a chapter of our life.

After the holidays, we went back to Venezuela. NTM would schedule me for flights based on the needs of individual missions and my work schedule. Depending on my destination, I would fly between 150–200 miles from Puerto Ayacucho to reach the outlying mission bases. With each trip, I became more confident flying over the Amazon. It is like flying over the ocean, but instead of a sea of blue, what you observe is a sea of green as far as your eye can see. I recorded each trip on my homemade map, noting any changes from previous trips. On several occasions, I had to divert my Cherokee 235 to another landing strip due to deteriorating weather, and the information on my map saved my life and my plane. I also had a mobile crystal radio installed on the plane to keep in touch with the mission bases.

Most of the mission airstrips had been laboriously cleared by hand, so they were short and bumpy. In most places, I had to take off and land within four hundred to six hundred feet. On one of the airstrips, I would fly off the end of the runway and follow the river while gaining enough altitude to make it over the trees. I always flew under the cloud cover to keep my bearings on the ground.

It was a big deal when I arrived at a mission base. As soon as the plane was on the ground and the engine shut down, natives, children, dogs, and the missionaries crowded around the plane to welcome me and help unload the cargo.

Some of the mission bases were far enough from Puerto Ayacucho that I could not fly to them and return without refueling. Besides what we used to reach missions, we used extra fuel for aerial surveys. New Tribes brought aviation fuel by boat from Puerto Ayacucho in 55-gallon drums. We had drop off locations to store the drums until needed. Gas deteriorates rapidly in the heat and high humidity of the Amazon, so filtering out water and sediment before use was critical. I made a special funnel to filter fuel into the tanks of the plane. We refueled by hand, several of us lifting the drum and pouring gas slowly into the funnel.

On several occasions, I flew people from the missions to Puerto Ayacucho for medical treatment. Of the two passengers that were the most seriously in need of help, one was a Piaroan boy that had been bitten by a poisonous snake and was not expected to live. Thanks to the anti-venom serum kept by the medical center in Puerto Ayacucho, he recovered completely.

The other person who needed emergency medical care was a young pregnant woman who had been in labor for several days and was not doing well. The flight was late in the day, and by the time I got the message, it was too dark to return to Puerto Ayacucho. I had no choice but to spend the night in the village, and by morning her condition had worsened. A Christian member of the local tribe accompanied the pregnant woman. It was foggy at first light, which was not uncommon due to the high humidity in the jungle. My first thought was to wait until the fog lifted, but given her critical condition, I decided to take off and trust the fog would clear with more altitude. With my two passengers huddled together in the back seats, I applied full power, and we bounced as we gained airspeed. Water droplets scattered on the windshield from the fog and high humidity. At seventy miles per hour, I lifted off and immediately lost sight of the runway. I stayed on my compass course, watching my rate of climb indicator and artificial horizon as we ascended through the fog. At nine hundred feet, I reduced flaps and prop pitch as the airspeed climbed to one hundred and ten miles per hour. At 1,500 feet, we broke out of the fog into a clear sky with the sun appearing over the horizon. What a beautiful sight—clear blue sky with the bright orange rays of the sunrise and the white cotton-field look of the fog below.

Someone from NTM headquarters was waiting for us when we landed in Puerto Ayacucho an hour and a half later. The pregnant woman and her friend were hurried off to the local medical clinic. The young woman gave birth to a boy, and both were healthy.

## PRINCIPLE ONE: PRAYER.

The first and foremost of the five principles is prayer. Daily communication with Jesus through the Holy Spirit is essential if we are to glorify God in all we think, say, and do. Philippians 4:6, "Do not be anxious about anything, but in every situation, by prayer and petition, with thanksgiving, present your requests to God." Throughout our married life, Dorothy and I have prayed without ceasing. Sometimes doors were closed; other times doors were opened. Sometimes we liked the answer, and sometimes we were disappointed. We learned that God always hears and answers our prayers in his time and his way for our good. Psalm 119:105, "Your word is a lamp for my feet, a light on my path." As we take one step at a time, we do not know where the path will lead us, but we know and trust who is leading.

I begin each day with prayer, petitions, and praise for what Jesus has done in my life and for those around me. Throughout the rest of the day, prayer is not an event, it is a natural part of my being. Like breathing, Jesus is the source of my spiritual life, without which I would surely die.

The Bible is filled with scriptures on prayer. The NIV translation of the Bible has 367 specific verses about prayer. How can I be sure God hears my prayers? First John 5:15, "And if we know that he hears us—whatever we ask—we know that we have what we asked of him." God answers prayers because he loved us enough to send his son Jesus Christ to die for us on the cross. When we take the time to pray, we acknowledge our dependence upon the Lord, and our understanding of him deepens. It is a proactive act of faith. He already knows exactly what we need before we ask.

Prayer is a two-way conversation. Continually asking and not listening is a one-way conversation. How much of your prayer life is asking for something instead of seeking God and his direction for your life? Beware you do not love the gifts more than the giver. Matthew 6:25–26, "Therefore I tell you, do not worry about your life, what you will eat or drink; or about your body, what you will wear. Is not life more than food, and the body more than clothes? Look at the birds of the air; they do not sow or reap or store away in barns, and yet your heavenly Father feeds them. Are you not much more valuable than they?" Our goal should be to see God's will carried out here on earth as well as in our personal lives as the Lord's Prayer in Matthew 6:9-13 reminds us:

"This, then, is how you should pray:
'Our Father in heaven,
hallowed be your name,
your kingdom come,
your will be done,
 on earth as it is in heaven.
Give us today our daily bread.
And forgive us our debts,
 as we also have forgiven our debtors.
And lead us not into temptation,
 but deliver us from the evil one.'"

In March 1970, I was talking to the manager of our Ford Tractor division, Robert Weiser, about my work with New Tribes, and the subject of the airstrip at TamaTama came up. Even though TamaTama was the home base for New Tribes in the Amazon Territory, it did not have an airstrip. Previous attempts to clear an airstrip close to the base confirmed that the chosen terrain was not suitable nor long enough. The terrain east of the base had enough length but would require mechanized equipment to clear the heavy forest and hilly terrain. Without an airstrip, all supplies were delivered to TamaTama by boat, a week-long trip from Puerto Ayacucho. Getting supplies to TamaTama was critical as it supported the outlying mission bases as well as a school for the missionary kids, a medical facility, radio communications, and administration for New Tribes work in the Territory.

A few minutes into the conversation about TamaTama and its needs, Bob offered, "Ford would be willing to donate a tractor if you can figure a way to get it there."

I was stunned at the magnitude of such a gift. It would mean so much to the New Tribes ministry.

"It would be a great marketing theme for us: 'Ford Tractor conquers the Amazon.' You have to find a way to get it there though." Bob was the consummate salesman, elegantly dressed and charismatic, truly a type A personality. I am not sure if he was enthused to help NTM, Ford, or both. The Lord works in strange ways, I thought. Who am I to question? I thanked Bob and said I would get back to him after I had worked out the details. I was excited as this tractor could be the answer to many prayers for an airstrip at TamaTama.

After a few days of praying and realizing there was no other way of moving a tractor five hundred miles into the Amazon Territory than by airlift, I talked to my good friend Captain Baroni. As a commercial pilot and a former Venezuelan air force pilot, he might have colleagues who could help. As it turned out, he still maintained contact with friends in the Venezuelan air force in Maracay and would see what might be possible via his acquaintances. A few days later, Captain Baroni called to tell me I was in luck. A friend at the military base in Maracay, thirty miles north of Valencia, said he would arrange for a flight in a Lockheed C-130 cargo plane that delivered supplies to Las Esmeraldas military outpost located on the Orinoco River about twenty-five miles east of TamaTama. They could take the tractor to this outpost, and we would only have to figure out how to move it from there up the Orinoco to TamaTama.

The flight was scheduled for April 10. I had not told the good news to the folks in TamaTama, so on my next trip to Puerto Ayacucho, I told Don Bodin how the Lord was working to provide a tractor for TamaTama. Of course, this announcement produced much joy and excitement.

Closer to the flight date, Captain Baroni let me know the plane would be leaving for Las Esmeraldas on April 10 as planned. He reminded me to have the tractor delivered to the Maracay military base before that date—as if I needed reminding! I contacted Bob Weiser to explain the logistics of getting the tractor to TamaTama. Bob admitted he had not thought the arrangements were really going to work, but he agreed to have the tractor delivered to the base in time. "Take lots of photos," Bob said.

I had been to Las Esmeraldas several times. This military outpost had the largest landing strip in the Amazon Territory, 2,000 feet, and proved a convenient landing stop in bad weather. On April 10, equipped with a camera, I flew to Las Esmeraldas to meet up with the transport plane, and sure enough, there was the C-130 on the ground surrounded by several people including Paul Dye, Jake Toews, others from NTM, and military officers. As I walked closer, I saw the tractor on the grass runway beside the plane. The C-130 has a cargo ramp that folds down from the back of the plane, and Jake had driven the tractor off and stopped it where it now stood.

Everyone was excited, even the military officers. Here was the first Ford tractor anyone had ever seen in the Amazon.

I wondered how they were going to make the last twenty-five miles, knowing that the last leg was their responsibility. Had they been able to solve the challenge? I should have known they would as Paul told me they had found a barge used by a construction company to bring supplies up-river. It just happened to be in the area the week the tractor arrived, and the owner said the missionaries could borrow it to move the tractor. Coincidence, or the hand of God? I know what Paul and the others, including myself, believed. With a large outboard-powered canoe tied to either side, the barge was moved to Las Esmeraldas and waited for the transfer of the tractor onto the barge.

Loading the tractor proved to be no easy task. To steady the barge, we tied it to trees on the shore. Then, we used heavy planks to form a loading ramp. Our hearts were pounding as Jake drove the tractor onto the ramp. One misstep and the tractor could be six feet down in the Orinoco River! The ramp was barely wide enough for the tractor; there was little room for error. Ever so carefully, Jake inched the tractor up the ramp. We held our breaths.

"Lord," I prayed, "if you want this tractor to do your work in TamaTama, help us get it on the barge."

Slowly, Jake steered the heavy tractor up our makeshift ramp. Then, finally, the front wheels and, after a minute, the back wheels rolled onto the barge. There was a big shout from everyone and celebratory hugs. The whole operation had made for a great photo shoot.

The TamaTama people were in a hurry to get back before dark, so we said goodbye and they shoved off. Watching the barge head upriver followed by two smaller boats that Paul and the others had arrived in, I prayed for their safe return and thanked God for these men and women who dedicated their lives to serving him. After they departed, I headed to Puerto Ayacucho for fuel and then home to Valencia. The C-130 had already departed for Maracay an hour earlier.

Flying back to Valencia, I could not help but think of the kindness of the people who had been involved to make this happen—some of whom I did not even know. The odds appeared insurmountable. Even our benefactor, Bob Weiser, was amazed and said to me, "Can you believe it? A Ford tractor in the Amazon!" I told him, "We serve a mighty God."

The takeaway is that God will use you to glorify his name no matter the circumstances. God kept me at Ford for a reason. There were people who had never heard the Gospel, missionaries that needed air support, and tractors to deliver. God coordinated Ford Motor Company, the Venezuelan Air Force, and a building contractor with a barge to carry out his purpose.

Being a Christian is not a spectator sport. We all long for and need a "mountain top" experience now and then, but we must return to the valley if we are to reach the lost. Each of us has a mission field wherever we are right now. It doesn't have to be faraway places; it can be people in your neighborhood or that you encounter at the grocery store. God will uniquely use you to touch someone that only you can reach. What an awesome responsibly and blessing!

Work on the airstrip in TamaTama began the second week of April and progressed quickly. On May 15, 1970, I made my first landing on the new runway. While it was still under construction, enough had been cleared for me to land safely. It was a thrill to see what had been done in such a short time with the help of the tractor. Jake Toews was primarily responsible for the layout and construction of the airstrip. In his fifties, Jake had been on the mission field for years and was a jack of all trades, an inventor, and above all, a joy to be around. It was my first time in TamaTama, and I stayed with Paul and Pat Dye and their children Larry and Lisa. They were great hosts, and I enjoyed seeing the facilities and meeting people I had heard of but never met. Several boats and canoes were lined up on the bank of the river for moving supplies. There was a shed nearby where outboard motors were stored and repaired. Fifty-five-gallon drums of gasoline were stored near the water's edge for the outboard motors, generators, and now my plane. TamaTama was also the radio communication and administrative center for the remote mission bases. To the outside world, this was basic living, but it was a metropolis compared to the mission outposts.

In June 1970, Carlos Medina called me into his office and explained he was resigning from the company. He had found a better executive position at another company in Caracas. He wanted me to hear it from him personally. Carlos had been a big help to Dorothy and me when we first got settled in Venezuela and after the plane crash in Maracaibo. There was not much I could say except I wished him the best and I would miss him. He already knew that based on our relationship. We shook hands, and he thanked me for the help. I never saw Carlos again, but I heard from mutual friends he was doing well.

I had just returned from my meeting with Carlos when the managing director, John Goulden, called to inform me I would be replacing Carlos as acting industrial relations director until a permanent replacement could be found.

Was I at risk of stepping into a job that was too big for me? Once again, I am amazed at how each of us are placed in circumstances that seem overwhelming, but with God in control all things are possible. Keep your focus on Jesus; he will take care of the rest.

My only mishap in 680 hours of flying in the Amazon was in June 1970 landing on a short rain-soaked airstrip. Dorothy and Paul and Pat Dye were with me. We were fully loaded, so I kept the airspeed up a bit on landing. A brief shower had just passed through the area, and I could tell when we touched down it would be difficult to stop on the wet grass. For an instant, time stood still as my mind raced for options. I was slowing down, but was it enough? I lowered the flaps on the wings to provide additional drag. Applying too much brake on the slippery grass could cause the plane to spin out of control. Then I felt the thump as we bounced over a small mound at the end of the runway and nosed into the bushes. As soon as the plane stopped, I shouted for everyone to get out quickly in case of fire. After we had exited the plane, I asked if everyone was alright. "Shaken but fine" was the answer. With the help of a few natives, we pushed the plane back onto the runway. Paul and I were apprehensive as we walked around the plane.

We were pleasantly surprised to find little damage—a few scratches and a slight bend of an inch on one of the two blades of the propeller. Flying with a propeller out of balance could create enough vibration to damage the motor and ought not be ignored. We tied a six-foot pole to the propeller with clothesline and applied light pressure. After repeated adjustments over several hours, we could see no difference between the two blades. Following a brief discussion, we decided that Dorothy and I would take off and, if there was no vibration, continue to Valencia. Paul and Pat would then return to TamaTama by boat. Two members of the local tribe were going down river toward TamaTama to hunt tapir and could drop Paul and Pat off on the way. TamaTama was a four-hour trip by boat and a thirty-minute jump by air.

We prayed together for a safe trip and said goodbye. Fortunately, I had refueled at Puerto Ayacucho on our way to pick up Paul and Pat at TamaTama, and I felt Dorothy and I could make the trip back to Valencia non-stop. After take-off, I listened carefully for vibration and was relieved when there was none. We experienced no problems on the four-and-a-half-hour trip home, landing in Valencia just before dark. On the way back, the realization of what had just happened began to sink in; Dorothy and I decided she would stay with Luanne and Dennis in the future. It was too risky for both of us to travel together. In case of an accident, we did not want our children to be orphans. After the fact, it seemed foolish we would have taken the risk of flying together; perhaps we had become too complacent of the dangers of flying in the Amazon. We were all too familiar with the tragic consequences of a plane crash.

With the new airstrip in TamaTama now available to me, I began aerial surveys south and east of TamaTama. In total, we flew 108 surveillance hours between May and November 1970. During that time, we spotted approximately fifteen huts and clearings previously unknown to the missionaries. We covered territory far to the south and east of TamaTama, near or over the Brazilian border. It would be fair to say much of the region had never been flown over by a small plane.

In October 1970, John Goulden informed me that my temporary assignment was over and that John Rinz would be the industrial relations director. I would return to my previous position as labor relations manager. John Goulden was pleased with my performance and had recommended I stay in the position. However, he had been overruled by Ford in Dearborn. I thanked John and told him I understood there were others in Ford who had earned the right to a promotion. I knew when doors were shut, the Lord had other plans. When I told Dorothy, she reacted as expected and simply said, "There is a good reason. We just don't know what it is yet."

# CHAPTER 4: LABOR STRIFE AND SAYING GOODBYE

*"Blessed are the peacemakers,*
*for they will be called children of God."*
*Matthew 5:9*

*Signing of Ford contract 7-24-71.*
*Sitting on right from top: Carvalho, Fresneda,*
*Blue, Rinz, and Sabainto; Jesus Perez setting in*
*white suit at end.*

When Rafael Caldera became president of Venezuela on December 1, 1968, it was the first peaceful transition of power in Venezuelan history. One of his early actions as president was to grant amnesty to clandestine guerrilla fighters who had been operating in the country the previous ten years. There was an undercurrent of political unrest between several political parties which Ford and other international companies would soon experience.

By early 1971, labor unrest in the country had increased. Most American companies located in Valencia, the center of industrial growth, had been threatened with a strike or were on strike, including Firestone, Goodyear, Celanese, General Motors, and Dana corporations. I knew most of the union officials at the Ford plant and at the national federation levels. Jesus Perez, the plant union chairman, was also an officer of Fetracarabobo and the Sindicato Sutra Automotriz Carabobo, national unions with international affiliations. We got along reasonably well, and I liked Jesus personally. Although he never showed it in public, I think the same could be said of his feelings for me.

January to April 1971 were focused on preparing for union negotiations. Miguel (Mike) Fresneda and I were busy bringing John Rinz up to date on key issues and developing a negotiating strategy. The next several months would be pivotal for Ford and the Venezuelan government in combating the growing labor unrest in the country.

John Rinz and I had developed a good working relationship during the five months before negotiations began, and most importantly, we had grown to trust each other. He accepted his grasp of Spanish and his knowledge of the labor situation in Venezuela were limited, so he recommended I take the lead in the negotiations when they began April 19. On my part, I depended on him to ensure management in Caracas and Dearborn understood the situation and were ready to support our efforts. Backing from upper management would be critical to fashion an agreement. The trust and respect John and I had for each other would grow significantly during the negotiations. My Spanish was good enough to participate, and it would become even better due to the never-ending discussions with the union and the government.

Wages and benefits were important issues to the unions, but several of the demands, sponsored by the national union, involved decision making and ownership of the company. Ford had become the battleground where discontent was fostered among the general population against international companies and the government.

John Rinz and I kept the Ministry of Labor, Nectario Labarca, informed of negotiations and our assessment with how the political situation was threatening the ability of Ford and other international companies to manage their business. The Minister of Labor did not want to appear to be taking sides and choose not to intervene. He preferred that Ford and the union continue negotiating to reach an agreement without intervention from the government. General labor unrest in the plant continued to escalate. Some workers attempted to sabotage operations. On June 3, after six weeks of discussions, negotiations broke down and the workers voted to go on strike. Mike and I sensed there was no serious intent on the part of the union to reach a settlement. We met with Jesus Perez and the union committee in a last effort to head off the strike but to no avail. Jesus confirmed what Mike and I had been thinking: the negotiation was now bigger than Ford and the company union. Other parties (the national union, opposition political parties, and left-wing activists) were now involved and controlling the situation. We kept the Ford administration building open to allow non-unionized salaried employees to continue working. After a few days, it became difficult for anyone to enter due to the protesters in front of the plant. We decided in the interest of safety to tell everyone except essential personnel to stay home until further notice.

Mike Fresneda was invaluable during the negotiations. Mike was born in Cuba and moved to Venezuela with his parents during the Castro revolution in the late 1950s. He was also an excellent baseball pitcher and had played professionally in Venezuela before coming to Ford. Fit and trim, always well dressed, with never a hair out of place, he looked the part of James Bond. Mike and I became close friends at work and socially, even playing on the company baseball team together.

Bob Copp, the director of labor relations for Ford Motor Company, and I talked almost daily on the status of negotiations and the strike. With no end in sight, Bob suggested it would be worth him coming to Venezuela if for no other reason than to get an on-site update. Top management was anxious to find a resolution. On June 17, I met Bob at the airport in Caracas. As we drove to Valencia, we discussed options and actions we might take to start talks with the union. Over the previous two weeks, I had reached out to both the Minister of Labor and the unions to restart talks. The union wanted concessions before starting talks again, all dealing with concession of management rights. Ford was not prepared to give up these management rights, and the Minister of Labor cautioned us if Ford capitulated our defeat would politically weaken the government.

Bob and I were in my office talking when the security supervisor came by and advised us of a large group of protesters moving down the street toward the plant. Unless we wanted to stay overnight, he suggested we leave before they got to us. I looked at Bob and said with a smile, "What do you think? You could get a first-hand update." Bob said, "Hell, no, let's get out of here." The security supervisor laughed, and said, "You better go while you can. I'm staying." Bob and I got in my car and drove out through the main entrance. You could see the crowd of seventy to eighty protesters coming toward the plant. As we drove out, the protestors shouted at us, but we kept on going.

I took Bob back to the Ford guest house where we had dinner together. We decided I would take him to the Ford Venezuela headquarters located in Caracas the next morning to confer with John Goulden as it was too risky to go back to the plant. Ford headquarters, located on several floors of a fifteen-story office building in downtown Caracas, were where our non-manufacturing functions such as finance, sales, marketing, and public relations were located to be close to the commercial center of the country. After an informative meeting with John Goulden, I took Bob to the airport. He told me as he was readying to board the flight home that he fully supported how we were handling the negotiations and would convey that to top management. He said he had no idea how difficult the situation had become until he had experienced it firsthand.

As the strike went on, it gave me pause for reflection. I knew God wanted me in Venezuela to assist NTM, but what about a prolonged labor strike involving the Venezuelan Government, Ford, and international unions? So many lives were being negatively impacted. I prayed for God to give me wisdom as a peacemaker and that my actions would glorify his name. One thing I knew for sure: I was not there by chance.

Threats against management and intimidation of workers became frequent in Valencia. With the plant closed due to the strike, we offered to relocate work assignments to our Ford headquarters in Caracas for all critical management and salaried employees who felt threatened and to provide them with temporary housing in the capital. Working in Caracas, they would not have to cross picket lines at the plant and risk physical harm. Some of these employees chose not to leave Valencia because they didn't feel threatened or because they expressed personal reasons for staying such as not taking their children out of school. We provided daily flights from Valencia to headquarters in Caracas for those who had to commute. Only personnel who were necessary to maintain equipment, utilities, and security services in the plant or involved in negotiations were required to remain in Valencia. I was given the option of moving Dorothy and the kids to Caracas, but she wanted to stay in Valencia with me. I encouraged John Rinz and his wife, Rita, to go to Caracas. His Spanish was too limited to be useful in negotiations, and I believed he could be more effective in Caracas near government offices. They agreed.

Everyone involved on the Ford side—both in Venezuela and in Dearborn—was evidently concerned about the strike. Jesus Perez and I met secretly a few times with no progress. It was apparent that the government was using Ford as a buffer against the left-leaning union movement for political reasons. The Minister of Labor was well aware of the political ramifications if the unions continued to make inroads in the control of foreign companies but for political reasons choose not to take sides publicly.

We were into our fourth week of the strike when public opinion began to turn against the union. Due to increasing pressure from the workforce and the general public, the union began to soften its demands.

On July 15, about six weeks into the strike, a clandestine meeting was held at the home of Dr. Luis Carvallo, the company attorney. Luis had been a prominent attorney for many years in Caracas and was highly regarded by business leaders and people in the government. His spacious home on several acres five miles from Valencia was the ideal venue for such a meeting—lots of room for guests, quiet surroundings, and security from outsiders. Twenty-two people attended including Jesus Perez and other union officials from state and international affiliates, government officials from the Ministry of Labor, and Ford representatives, Dr. Carvallo, Mike Fresneda, and me. There was an armed guard outside the door to ensure all present were invited guests; several attendees carried handguns including Dr. Carvallo. I was not armed. You could feel the tension—no smiles or handshakes. My college degree was in labor economics, and I do not recall this being covered in the class on union-management relations. The stakes were high for everyone—the union, the company, and the government. The meeting lasted until well after midnight. Finally, an agreement was reached, and there were sighs of relief from all sides and even some handshakes and smiles as we left the meeting. It was two a.m. when I called John Rinz in Caracas to inform him of the settlement. John did not mind my calling him at that early hour; I could hear the relief in his voice as we talked. He said he would wait to inform Mr. Goulden so as not to disturb him. John and I had agreed it was best for him and his wife to stay in Caracas during the negotiations due to the personal threats against Ford management in Valencia, but now that an agreement had been reached, it was important for him to return to Valencia to participate in the signing ceremony on behalf of Ford.

A three-year collective bargaining agreement was officially signed on July 20, 1971, at the Ford plant in Valencia. Details and photos of the signing were headlined in the two largest newspapers, El Carabobeno in Valencia and El Globo in Caracas. Had we not held our ground, I believe the future political and labor situation in Venezuela would have been tenuous. We had arrived at a fair contract for all sides, including a signing bonus for the employees. Most importantly for us, our management rights were still intact. I thanked God for the equitable outcome for all participants. In spite of all the rancor, God's grace had prevailed.

With the help of the media and word of mouth, we notified our workforce of 1,600 employees that the plant would reopen on July 23. Because there was still opposition to the agreement from some factions within the union and left-wing political organizations, Mike and I felt there might be trouble reopening the plant. We alerted local law enforcement, who were under the control of the Ministry of Defense due to the political unrest in the country, of the possibility of protests, and we asked them to be prepared to assist us if necessary. On July 23, 1971, when a crowd of about five hundred people gathered outside the main entrance to the plant, our security officers told us only a few of the protesters were Ford employees. Most of the others were agitators from various opposition groups. After discussion with the local law enforcement authorities, John and I decided against opening the plant. Someone could get hurt, and we wanted to avoid damage to the plant. We made announcements to the employees at the gate and through the media that we would open the plant the next morning. The local police were not equipped to handle the large crowd. The police chief and John, Mike, and I decided jointly to contact the Guardia National, a branch of the Venezuela military that handles threats to internal security, to request their help. The commandant of the Guardia National told us by phone he was already aware of our situation, but he did not say from whom. He agreed to send sixty elite troops to spend the night at the plant. Several of our production managers, security personnel, and John, Mike, and I also stayed at the plant and prepared for the worst. We had cots to sleep on and coffee and sandwiches prepared by the cafeteria for everyone staying at the plant during the night.

Following a sleepless night, John, Mike, and I gathered in John's office on the second floor of the administration building around six a.m. the next morning. By seven a.m., a crowd of around seven hundred protestors had formed outside the main entrance shouting and waving banners denouncing Ford. Another group of about three hundred Ford employees, anxious to return to work, stood apart from the protestors waiting for the main gate to open at eight a.m. The security office at the main entrance was staffed with six security guards, but they were no match for the crowds. The protestors were getting unruly and began pushing against the cyclone fence in front of the plant. From our vantage point on the second floor of the administrative building, one hundred yards from the main entrance, Mike and I could tell the fence would soon go down, so we alerted the Guardia National, already stationed inside the plant, to be prepared. I had just looked at my watch to check the time; it was 7:35 a.m. when the fence suddenly collapsed. The angry protesters charged toward the plant. Simultaneously, the Guardia National troops emerged from the plant and confronted the protestors about halfway between the main gate and entrance to the plant. The troops, dressed in dark green combat uniforms, helmets, and boots and carrying batons and automatic weapons, engaged the protestors with precision, swinging their batons while other troops fired automatic weapons into the sky. The noise of the shouting and the gunfire was surreal; I saw everything in slow motion. Then, after just a few minutes, it was over. A few stunned protestors remained on the ground; the others were running back toward the main gate. It was obvious these troops were experienced in quelling riots. There were some arrests, and the protestors soon dispersed. We attended to a few of the injured in our plant medical facility. Thankfully, no one was seriously hurt.

With the help of Ford security guards, the Ford employees who had gathered outside the gate were advised to sign in at the gate house and return to work the next morning. We told them they would be paid for the day of the riot. Temporary repairs were made to the fence in preparation to reopen the plant again the next morning. The commander of the Guardia National felt reopening the next day would not allow time for the protestors to regroup. The following morning, with the Guardia National troops stationed outside the main entrance, approximately five hundred employees returned to work. A group of protestors, perhaps one hundred, stood to one side of the main entrance shouting and waving banners but allowing employees to pass through the main gate. There was some pushing and shoving at the gate, but no one was hurt or arrested. With this, we knew we were on our way to normalizing our operation once again. It took about a week to finally reach full production. I can remember talking with John Rinz and Mike Fresneda one day after it was all over and thinking, "Did this really happen?" I took the opportunity to remind them, "With God all things are possible." Knowing my Christian beliefs, John and Mike collectively said, "AMEN." We were all drained emotionally and physically but had become comrades under trying circumstances. It was also the beginning of the end of labor strife in the country for the coming years. Jesus Perez stayed on as union chairman and eventually went on to become a member of the national Venezuelan congress. Mike Fresneda was promoted to replace me as labor relations manager when I left to return to the US four months later in November 1971. John Rinz stayed on for an additional two years before returning to the US, and Mike then replaced him as industrial relations director. It was a unique and memorable experience to end my work at Ford Venezuela.

During 1971, I continued to make trips as often as I could for New Tribes, knowing that my assignment in Venezuela was to end soon. I had made overtures to the company to say that I would be willing to stay in Venezuela for additional time but to no avail. John, and the management in Dearborn, felt there were better opportunities for me elsewhere in the company. That turned out to be true, but none of the "better" assignments kindle the memories we have of Venezuela. We lost John and Lucille but took so much with us: spiritual growth, life-long friends, and memoires of working with New Tribes Mission, of worshipping at The Fellowship Church, and most of all, of the birth of our son Dennis.

In August 1971, there was a knock on the door of our home in Valencia. It was Padre Sanchez who, having retired from the mission in Las Esmeraldas, was on his way home to Spain. He wanted to say goodbye and thank me for all I had done for him while I was at Las Esmeraldas. I invited him in. He could only stay briefly, but he talked with delight about the day the Ford tractor arrived and how he would miss Las Esmeraldas where he had ministered to the native tribes for twenty years. I asked him to stay for dinner, but he declined. We hugged—a big abrazo—and he left. After three years immersed in Spanish-language culture, my ability to read, write, and converse in Spanish was more than adequate. It would serve me well in learning Portuguese on a future assignment.

As fall 1971 approached and my time to leave Venezuela was proximate, I sold my plane to a friend of Captain Baroni in Caracas, to be delivered after my last trip to TamaTama on September 10, 1971. It was difficult saying goodbye to so many I had grown to love and respect. I recalled how I would feel guilty when I left one of the remote mission bases to fly back to my much easier life in Valencia. Leaving behind these dedicated families to

58

labor under such difficult conditions did not seem fair. One day, I was relating this to Joe Dawson, and he said to me how blessed and privileged they were to be called to serve the Lord under any circumstances and did not want to be anywhere else.

Flying home to Valencia that last time on September 10, 1971, my mind drifted back to May 1963 when I first met Dorothy, our marriage, John having a plane, my passion for flying, doors closing at Eastern Airlines and Campus Crusade, my career at Ford, my transfer to Venezuela, the tragic plane crash in Maracaibo, and my first meeting with Don Bodin, Jim Bou, and Paul Dye to lay out a plan for me to fly for NTM. It had been a long and sometimes difficult journey that had brought me here. Was it chance, coincidence, or the hand of God directing us over the past eight years? Even for the skeptical, the odds would seem astronomical. I cannot explain it, but I am reminded of Hebrews 11:1, "Now faith is confidence in what we hope for and assurance about what we do not see." What I do know is that Dorothy and I lived it, the gentle nudging of the Holy Spirit to open and close doors, the strength to endure difficulties and heartbreak, praise for the many blessings, and the peace of knowing God is in control.

It seems like yesterday when I made my first flight to Puerto Ayacucho, but considering the many memories: the Yuwana contact, aerial surveys, medical emergencies, supply deliveries, close calls, and, of course, the Ford tractor, I know better. Based on my flight log, I flew 680 hours in eighteen months for New Tribes; I was privileged to have played a small part in bringing the gospel to the Amazon. I can still smell the pungent odor of unclean bodies and sweat, smoke, and dirt inside the tribal shabanos (huts), the bites of the insects, and the rituals of the witchdoctor trying to appease the spirits on behalf of a sick or lost loved one. I wished it did not have to end but knew that the Lord had other things in store for us. By design, I was never reimbursed for fuel and maintenance nor paid for my time flying for New Tribes. It was God's work; I could never repay him. Matthew 28:19–20, "Therefore, go and make disciples of all nations, baptizing them in the name of the Father and the Son and the Holy Spirit, and teaching them to obey everything I have commanded you."

In 2005, Hugo Chavez, President of Venezuela, announced he was expelling New Tribes Mission from Venezuela, accusing the organization of imperialism and working for the CIA. On November 5, 2005, hundreds of Venezuelan indigenous people marched in Puerto Ayacucho against the government expulsion of NTM but to no avail. Since 1946, New Tribes had served the indigenous communities in Venezuela through translation, church planting, literacy, humanitarian aid, and community development programs in Amazonas Territory. NTM had worked with twelve ethnic groups, nine with established churches, and completed five Bible translations. Four other translations were in progress.

From a work perspective, the previous three years were an invaluable learning experience. What started out to be a six-month assignment to revise company benefit programs turned into a far-reaching exposure to every aspect of a corporate career. I experienced changes in title, job description, managing directors, and immediate supervisors. My experiences would serve me well on my return to Dearborn.

# CHAPTER 5: DOWN UNDER IN AUSTRALIA

*"I know that you can do all things; no purpose of
yours can be thwarted." Job 42:2*

*Dennis with a 719-pound black marlin
in Cairns, Australia, 1973.*

We returned to Michigan in November 1971 and moved into
a Ford Motor Company apartment in Dearborn while we looked for
a house. It was good to be home and share our lives with family and
friends, but we missed Venezuela. We drove through our old
neighborhood in Farmington and then to Kimberly Subdivision
where John and Lucille had lived. The house had been sold to new

owners but looked the same from the outside. We stopped in front and sat quietly recalling our happy times together as we had the last time we were inside. It was plausible to imagine knocking on the door and greeting John and Lucille; they would have been so glad to see us and the grandkids! It was good to connect with Ron and Ina, our first opportunity since their visit to Venezuela in April 1970. Their children, Ronda and John, had grown since we saw them last.

I had been on my new job for a month as special studies analyst, foreign services administration, when my manager, Harry Craig, called me into his office. He had news: Ford wanted to offer me a promotion to labor relations and personnel services manager, Ford Asia Pacific, in Melbourne, Australia. Ford Asia Pacific had been formed in 1970 to oversee and expand Ford operations in the rapidly growing Asian market. In 1972, its new headquarters was established in Melbourne, and I was fortunate to be part of the initial staffing. This was to be a four-year assignment.

Bob Mahon, director of human resources, Ford Asia Pacific, would be in Dearborn in December and wanted to discuss the position with me. I was pleasantly surprised. I had no idea the offer was coming. This foreign-service assignment rekindled a spark for life overseas. I liked my current job but not in comparison to Venezuela and the broader scope of my responsibilities there.

I could not wait to tell Dorothy to see her reaction. She was both surprised and a little apprehensive. "Do we really want to pack up and move again with two small children?" she asked. "We'll be gone for four years!" The easy—and perhaps reasonable—thing would be to settle into my job in Dearborn, find a house and a church in suburbia, and raise our family stateside. In addition, Ron and Ina would be disappointed as they had anticipated having us nearby and watching our kids grow up together. Dorothy and I wondered if this opportunity had a spiritual purpose. We have learned that oftentimes commonsense is not faith and faith not commonsense. There are numerous examples in the Bible of God using secular institutions and events to further his purposes such as using Egypt to provide for Jacob's family during the famine or the wise men from the East bringing resources for Joseph, Mary, and Jesus so they could move to Egypt and escape Herod the Great's massacre of male children in Bethlehem. Dorothy and I reminded one another how, early in our marriage, we felt a calling to the Campus Crusade ministry, but God closed the door on our attempt to leave Ford. After our time with Ford and New Tribes in Venezuela, we understood why. This opportunity to move to Australia might be God's calling to another ministry. After talking it over, we decided to pray about it. If God opened the door, we would accept the promotion.

Just before Christmas, Bob Mahon was up from Australia to discuss the promotion. Bob told me that, based on my work in Venezuela, I was highly recommended by Ford management and he was looking for someone who could think "outside of the box." Ford Asia Pacific was launching new affiliates and facilities in countries where established Ford policies were not the norm. Bob informed me that revising polices and work practices to fit local circumstances would be key to the success of these launches. During this conference, I confirmed that I would take the position, and we agreed on a March departure date. I immediately advised Dorothy I had accepted the position, and she confirmed what I was already feeling: God was calling us to another ministry in Australia. This would be an affirmation of the decision we made to return to Venezuela after the tragic death of John and Lucille.

Little did we know we would spend the next ten years moving between Australia, New Zealand, and Brazil before returning home in 1982. I learned the meaning of John 17:16, "They are not of this world, even as I am not of it." We are all born into this world and become a citizen of a country. If you accept Jesus Christ into your life, then you have been born again. John 3:3–7, Jesus replied, "Very truly I tell you, no one can see the kingdom of God unless they are born again." "How can someone be born when they are old?" Nicodemus asked. "Surely they cannot enter a second time into their mother's womb to be born!" Jesus answered, "Very truly I tell you, no one can enter the kingdom of God unless they are born of water and the Spirit. Flesh gives birth to flesh, but the Spirit gives birth to spirit. You should not be surprised at my saying, 'You must be born again.'"

As US citizens living outside the US, we were resident aliens and subject to the authority of that country. In the same manner, as Christians we are resident aliens here on Earth, subject to government authority. Romans 13:1, "Let everyone be subject to the governing authorities, for there is no authority except that which God has established. The authorities that exist have been established by God." Our citizenship is of the Kingdom of God and subject to his ultimate authority. One thing that does not change here on earth or in heaven is our relationship with God through Jesus Christ.

During my three and a half years in the Ford Asia Pacific region, I travelled extensively between our affiliate companies in Taiwan, Japan, the Philippines, Thailand, New Zealand, and Brazil.

My first meaningful project was a new assembly plant in Taipei, Taiwan. In June 1973, I was invited by Managing Director Ray Chen and Industrial Relations Director Don Vicary to the inauguration of the new plant near Taipei. I had been intimately involved in developing employment practices with Ray, Don, and government officials. Government regulations required Ford to provide employee living quarters, medical facilities, and all meals.

Two of my favorite projects were a consumer electronic plant at Manus, Brazil, and a stamping plant on the Bataan Peninsula in the Philippines, both in the middle of nowhere! The logistics and ingenuity to complete these projects were challenging and rewarding. My knowledge and experience of Ford worldwide operations had expanded exponentially. By necessity, I had been involved in numerous aspects of the company—beyond industrial relations—that would serve me well in the future.

Dorothy and I loved each of the countries we lived in for different reasons: Australia, big and diverse with unlimited potential as a nation; New Zealand, scenic, egalitarian, and as they say more British than the British; Brazil, friendly, hardworking, and fun loving. We made numerous lifelong friends in each country, both Christian and non-Christian, and several of which we stay in touch with today. Saying goodbye was the most difficult part of moving, but it was a price we gladly paid for the friendships made.

During our travels we attended Baptist, Presbyterian, and interdenominational churches. Dorothy and I were still members of the United Missionary Church back home; however, our experience moving between churches and denominations reaffirmed that it is not the name on the building but a personal relationship with Jesus Christ and his teaching that matters. As believers, we are members of the Body of Christ, yet this does not diminish the role of the organized church.

Not to be left out, I indulged my passion for fishing now and then. I caught a seven-hundred-pound Black Marlin and a record Northern Bluefin Tuna in Australia, brown and rainbow trout in the beautiful rivers of New Zealand, and huge peacock bass in Brazil. These were exotic places I never would have fished had it not been for my travels with Ford. I am still not sure if God was using me to pursue my passion to make disciples or go fishing—or both!

Growing up on a farm with no running water gave me my adventurous pioneer spirit and love of the outdoors. I fished for bullhead and carp in the creeks and ponds around the farm and, as I got older, went on trips to Lake Erie and Canada with my dad. A quote from Henry David Thoreau says it best, "Many men go fishing all of their lives without knowing that it is not fish they are after."

With John and Lucille gone, my mother was the only parent we had left. Ann had been a widow almost ten years and had established a new life for herself. She was now living in a one-bedroom apartment in a senior citizen's apartment building in

Riverview, Michigan, and had many elderly friends and activities to keep her busy. She had also found a church that she enjoyed near her apartment. Mom did her own cooking, but those residents who didn't want to cook could arrange for meals in a central dining room at an additional cost. She still drove and had her car outside in the apartment parking lot. My brother Tom, his wife Joann, and several neighbors kept in close touch with Mom in case of an emergency. It was good to know she could live there and remain independent.

Company policy required we purchase furniture in Australia rather than ship our own due to the high cost of transportation to and from Australia. It also made preparing to move much simpler. Our furniture from Venezuela was still in storage with Palmer Moving and Storage in Dearborn, where John and Lucille's furniture was also stored. We would not see this furniture again until we arrived home in 1982. On March 1, 1972, three and a half months after arriving in Michigan for what we had thought would be a long stay, we departed for Australia.

We found a new two-story detached condo on Port Phillip Bay, a thirty-minute drive east of Melbourne. It was just what we were looking for with only three other condos in a small cul-de-sac in Sandringham, a suburb of Melbourne. There was a community swimming pool which all condo residents enjoyed. One of our neighbors, Mike and Susan, were from England. Mike was a well-known celebrity on national TV and a singer. All the kids were within two years' age of each other and got along great together.

Luanne and Dennis and the neighbor kids went to Firbank Primary School, three blocks from where we lived. All students were required to wear uniforms sold by the school and were taught proper etiquette. We sent pictures to Grandma Blue and some of our friends. Everyone thought Luanne and Dennis looked so cute in their uniforms and hats. The kids settled in quickly and liked their new friends. It did not take them long to pick up an Aussie accent.

I still had an interest in flying and tested for my Australian pilot's license, as I thought there might be a chance to continue mission aviation in Australia. I determined most of the mission work was in New Guinea and northern Australia, over 1,500 miles from Melbourne. Beside the distance of the missions, another impediment was the amount of time I was required to travel on my job.

I logged only ten hours of flying time in a leased airplane over a period of six months after getting my license in Australia— not enough to stay proficient. I came to realize my real joy—and my intent—was fulfilling God's purpose. I understood flying was a means to an end. Without a specific purpose—missionary work— my enthusiasm to fly was no longer there.

## PRINCIPLE TWO: PURPOSE.

In one sense, as a Christian you are always living in God's purpose. God works all things, including your life, according to his purpose. At first, Dorothy and I struggled to find a personal Christian ministry in Australia—whether in a church, missions, or elsewhere. Then it occurred to us: we came to Australia believing that was where God wanted us; we were already fulfilling his purpose. The world is a mission field, and there are people all around us who need to hear the Word of God. Our mission field would be our neighbors, Bible studies, and whomever we contacted at work or in our personal lives.

A Christian's presence in the workplace provides the most natural and, at the same time, most overlooked opportunity to witness. Our work mindset should be neither idolatrous nor utilitarian. Instead, work as worship embraces the daily call to love our neighbors at our specific workplaces. My work and extensive travel around the world reinforced the need to bring my faith to work. We can all participate in the work mission field to the glory of God.

Do not confuse work with purpose. If we remain faithful and focused on Christ, He will use us to serve his purpose, whatever and wherever that may be. God wants you to be available so he can carry out his purpose through you. God will determine the when, where, and how of the work for you to achieve his purpose. We spend time setting goals, keeping busy, and worrying about things we cannot control when all God wants is for us to keep our focus on him. Colossians 3:23–24, "Whatever you do, work at it with all your heart, as working for the Lord, not for human masters, since you know that you will receive an inheritance from the Lord as a reward. It is the Lord Christ you are serving."

One of the items on my bucket list was to fish in Cairns, Australia, a town of 45,000 in 1972 that grew rapidly to 150,000 in the ensuing years. Located on the Great Barrier Reef, the largest coral reef system in the world, Cairns is 1,750 miles north of Melbourne. It has a tropical climate with miles of white sandy beaches.

The morning of September 18, 1973, I went fishing in Cairns with two friends from Melbourne. I was fortunate to book Captain Laurie Woodbridge on *Sea Baby II*, the top boat in Cairns. By mid-morning, my friends Jack and Art had released black marlins, 300 pounds each. "Too small to keep," said Captain Laurie. It was my turn; we had just set lines when a small marlin took the left flat line but did not hook up. Three hours passed without another bite; and the seas were getting rougher, ten feet and building. You could sometimes see marlin surfing in the large waves behind the boat as they came in to inspect the bait and then move away. Suddenly, Laurie shouted, "Big marlin in the spread, right rigger!" The first mates—Captain Laurie had two on the boat—sprang into action reeling in other lines while I grabbed the rod attached to the right outrigger, leaving it in the rod holder. The 130-pound mono line started screaming off the Penn Reel. After what seemed like a long time but was only fifteen seconds, Laurie shouted, "Set the drag!" I pushed the drag lever on the side of the reel to the strike setting. The line came tight, and the stout rod bent from the strain. Within seconds, a huge black marlin broke water one hundred and fifty feet behind the boat. I reduced drag and moved the rod into the fighting chair where the mate helped me attach the bucket harness to the reel. You sit on a bucket harness, much like a padded leather seat that extends up your lower back. Straps from the harness are clipped to the reel with the rod butt placed in a gimble on the fighting chair. The fish jumped again, breaking the surface by at least four feet. We fought the fish for about an hour as I increased drag and slowly put line back on the reel.

Captain Laurie backed down in reverse several times to take the pressure off the fish and help me gain line. Suddenly, there it was twenty feet behind the boat. A sight I will never forget, the iridescent blue of the fish silhouetted against the deep blue of the sea. The mate took the leader and guided the fish closer to the boat. This is a critical period when the mate, angler, and captain must be synchronized; a mistake can mean the loss of the fish or worse yet serious injury. There have been numerous broken bones and lost fingers handling these giant fish. The second mate gaffed the fish behind the dorsal fin, and water erupted as the leader man struggled to maintain control of the fish. A rope attached the gaff to a cleat while the mate lassoed the tail of the fish to the boat. After a brief struggle, the fish was ours. As we pulled the fish through the transom door, I could not believe its size. Captain Laurie estimated the fish at 700 to 750 pounds, approximately 12 feet long. There were high fives all around for a great catch. Back at the dock, the fish weighed in at 719 pounds. Today, catch and release is practiced by anglers. We are responsible to care for God's creatures and preserving the species through proper fisheries management should always be the goal. Captain Laurie Woodbridge went on to be inducted into the International Game Fish Association Hall of Fame in Fort Lauderdale, Florida.

# CHAPTER 6: BERMAGUI, A FISHERMAN'S PARADISE

*"Many are the plans in a person's heart,*
*but it is the Lord's purpose that prevails."*
*Proverbs 19:21*

*(left to right) Dennis, Dorothy, Luanne and*
*Dennis in Bermagui, Australia, 1975.*

Life in Australia was good. Dorothy and I made many friends and travelled often within that beautiful country. My mom came twice to visit us and the kids. She, too, enjoyed Australia—sightseeing around Melbourne and the countryside. We teased her about becoming a world traveler, first Venezuela and now Australia.

I had just returned from my fishing trip in Cairns when I got a call from Jeff Lovett at the St. Kilda Marina near our home in Melbourne. He had a used twenty-five-foot Bertram with twin 165 horsepower gas inboards and outdrives, and he wanted to know if I would be interested in trading in my twenty-foot Bertram, purchased from Jeff last year, along with a few extra dollars, for his boat. How could I resist? Dorothy agreed the trade was a great idea, so in October 1973 we became the owners of a new boat. I docked the boat at St. Kilda Marina and fished Port Phillip Bay for red snapper. Jeff told me about the excellent yellowfin fishing on Montague Island near Bermagui. Located on the continental shelf, ten miles north of Bermagui and nine miles offshore, Montague Island is home to some of the best yellowfin fishing in the world. As with Cairns, I wanted to try it, so Dorothy, the kids, and I took a weekend trip to Bermagui in November to check it out.

It was eight hours and 420 miles by car from Melbourne to Bermagui—a long way for a weekend trip—but the possibility of giant yellowfin made it seem worthwhile. Bermagui was a beautiful little fishing village overlooking the Indo-Pacific Ocean with about six hundred residents. There was one hotel with a restaurant and a pub, one motel, a few general stores, a campground, and another restaurant that was noted for its excellent seafood. There was no marina for recreational boats, only two long wharfs for the commercial fishing boats. Fishermen sold their catch of tuna, yellowtail, and mackerel to the fishermen's co-op, which then processed the fish for shipment to wholesalers. In total, there were fifteen commercial boats docked in the small harbor.

As we walked around town, I noticed one of the boats unloading its catch on the wharf and walked down for a closer look. Two men were lifting boxes of small tuna—both bluefin and yellowtail—onto a cart and taking them to the co-op at the end of the wharf. I introduced myself and complimented them on their catch. While they finished unloading, we exchanged pleasantries.

One of the men was Captain Johnny Cudd who had been fishing these waters since he was a kid and had just recently purchased his own boat. He was in his mid-thirties and married, but he had no children. I asked if he knew where I might dock a twenty-five-foot boat to use on weekends. He said most of the recreational fishermen kept their boats on trailers, and he knew of no recreational docking in the area. He added that he and a few other captains occasionally took paid customers to catch yellowfin.

As we were leaving the dock, I asked him how the restaurant was in town. He replied, "Great! My wife Shirley works there." He was going there himself for dinner and suggested we could eat together. He would introduce us to Shirley. The place was packed; fortunately, Shirley had reserved a table for us. The seafood was excellent: fish, oysters, scallops, abalone—you name it, they had it, fresh from the sea. Shirley was a pretty lady, pleasantly plump, with a friendly smile and disposition.

Johnny and I talked over dinner about fishing, and as we were about to leave, Johnny said, "I have been thinking. I have a seventy-foot section along the wharf and only need about forty feet of it for my boat. The boat in front of me has room to spare. I think you could dock between us and not be in the way."

That began almost two years of friendship and adventure with Johnny and his brother Phil and launched a new episode in our family's life. We spent most of our free time and vacations in Bermagui. Our normal routine was to leave Melbourne around six p.m. after work on Friday and arrive in Bermagui by two a.m. Saturday. I was up in the morning at six a.m. and fished hard until Sunday afternoon before driving the eight hours back to Melbourne Sunday night. Monday morning, I was back to work. Dorothy and the kids really enjoyed the weekends. They could sleep on the way to Bermagui and then relax over the weekend, swimming, sightseeing, fishing, or hanging out on the beach. It was a tiring weekend with little sleep for me, but the thrill of catching yellowfin tuna kept the adrenalin flowing. Dorothy would occasionally drive on the way home if I was overly tired, but after a good night's sleep, I was ready to go again on Monday. I had the energy of a young man.

It did not take long to realize we needed a place to call home in Bermagui. Lugging personal items back and forth was work, and we always left something behind. There was a trailer park overlooking the ocean that would make a perfect location for a house trailer we could call home on the weekends. In January 1974, we purchased a twenty-eight-foot Mallard house trailer that slept six and had a kitchen, toilet, and dinette. It was just right for our needs.

I would let Johnny know when I was coming for the weekend, and he would have live bait on my boat when I arrived in Bermagui. Johnny also provided us with fresh oysters. I remember shucking and eating oysters by the dozens with Luanne as we enjoyed the sweet salt-water taste right out of the sea.

Over the next two years, I caught many bluefin and yellowfin tuna. Not only were they fun to catch, but they had a high commercial value as seafood. I gave all my fish to Johnny to sell to the fishermen's co-op—a quid pro quo for my dockage and all he did for us. My biggest northern bluefin tuna of 59 pounds was certified by the Australia Gamefish Association as a record for that species caught on thirty-pound test line. My biggest yellowfin tuna was 131 pounds on twenty-pound breaking line. Not a record, but still my biggest yellowfin tuna.

In June 1974, Bob Mahon was transferred back to the US and was replaced by Hunter Pickens as human resources director. Hunter was a "good old boy" from Texas. Tall and lean, soft spoken and highly regarded by his peers in the company, he and his wife Pat were as happy to be in Australia as we were to have them.

Ford New Zealand had been experiencing labor problems the past year, and in March 1975, Hunter and I met to discuss how to address the deteriorating situation. The Ford New Zealand industrial relations director had retired in November 1974 after twenty years of service rather than battle the unions. He was replaced by Vance Hainsworth, a New Zealander by birth, who was an experienced industrial relations director from outside Ford.

Vance and I talked numerous times on the phone, but I wanted to see firsthand how things were going, so I made a quick three-day trip to Wellington in April 1975. Vance met me at the airport and took me directly to the Captain Cook Hotel where I was staying. Vance was in his forties, married, with two children in college. He reminded me of a college professor, six-foot tall and dressed in a brown wool suit with vest, slightly bald and grey around the temples. He was very proper in his manners and speech. I liked him right away. We talked over dinner that evening and got to know each other.

When I got home from New Zealand, I told Dorothy I had a feeling—call it what you will—that our assignment in Australia might be coming to an end. I have had these premonitions before and have learned to recognize the gentle nudging of the Holy Spirit. We decided to sell the Bertram and house trailer just in case we did leave Australia. I kept Johnny and Phil Cudd informed of what we were doing and why. They were disappointed they might lose us but understood our decision. I told them if it turned out we were staying in Australia they could help me find a bigger boat.

During 1974, I travelled outside Australia for a total of nine months, including several multiweek trips to Japan preparing for the launch of a new assembly facility in Yokohama. The Japanese people are orderly and friendly. They believe regulations are necessary, and without them, there would be chaos. Everything has a purpose, so they obey the rules. Writing and editing several hundred pages of Rules of Employment, Wage Rules, and Local Practices for approval by Ford of Japan, Ford Motor Company, and the Japanese Government was a monumental task. It was by far the most tedious and most rewarding of my career. I also grew in my understanding of Perspective and Patience, two of the biblical principles I discuss in this book. I kept in touch with my good friend, Anglos Lindsey, who was the industrial relations director at the time. We remained good friends and kept in touch after I left Australia. Anglos called me from the Ford Hospital in October 1982, shortly after I returned to Dearborn. He was seriously ill from cancer and wanted to say goodbye. The following day we spent time together at the hospital reminiscing about Japan and how blessed we had been with family and friends. I learned several days later from his wife that he had passed away.

One of the highlights of my time in Ford Asia Pacific was my work in Mariveles in the Philippines. Ford already had an assembly operation in Manila when President Fernando Marcos had established a tax-free manufacturing zone on the Bataan Peninsula in September 1972. The stampings would be provided to other Ford affiliates throughout the Asia Pacific region and improve the balance of trade for the Philippines.

I was assigned to help develop policies and staffing for the new facility. Ben Magnay, the industrial relations manager, was a Filipino by birth, spoke fluent English, and was one of our best affiliate industrial relations managers.

On my first trip to Manila, Ben met me at the airport and took me to my hotel. Ben was exactly like I pictured him on the phone: five-foot, six-inches, one-hundred and forty pounds, with black hair and glasses. He talked rapidly in a staccato fashion between smiles and laughs—a high energy, type A personality. On the way to the hotel, I was fascinated by the number of brightly decorated Jeepneys, a WWII version of the Jeep, and motorcycles with a side car that plied the streets as taxis. In the 1970s, Manila was a bustling city with more than one million residents and numerous suburbs surrounding the downtown district. The port of Manila is one of the largest in Asia with facilities stretching from the city for several miles on Manila Bay.

At seven a.m. the following morning, Ben and I drove to Mariveles. The road was a two-lane, part asphalt, part dirt road that was gutted with potholes. The area was desolate, consisting of a few small villages and farms and not much else. It took six hours to travel the 107 miles around Manila Bay to Mariveles. This road was so rough that it was impassible after a heavy rain. Mariveles is only thirty-five miles across the bay from Manila, and the distance can be easily negotiated in one hour on a high-speed ferry from Manila. Ben said he deliberately wanted me to go by road to experience the difficulty in transportation and logistics from Manila. Having given me his lesson for the day, Ben took me back on the ferry.

Establishing a facility in Mariveles was a large undertaking as we had to build a state-of-the-art stamping plant and provide infrastructure for a small community. We needed roads, housing for employees, a medical facility, stores, and schools. Most of the employees would come from outside the area and would eventually settle there. In March 1973, Ford broke ground on the new stamping plant in Mariveles.

My last trip to Mariveles was in May 1975. The facilities were almost completed, and I could tell it was going to be a first-class operation. The medical facility was state of the art. It included an operating room and was equipped to handle everyday medical care, trauma cases, and everything in between. Housing was mostly completed with people already living in the apartments and houses. Hiring and training the workforce had begun, and supervisors, skilled trades people, and numerous support staff were being trained on site. Ben and I kept in touch after I left Australia to discuss issues that would come up. The plant opened in early 1976.

On September 10, 1975, the feeling I had about leaving Australia came true. Hunter called me to his office to ask if I would be interested in replacing Vance in New Zealand. Ralph Fawcett, the managing director of Ford New Zealand, had called Hunter and requested Vance be replaced as soon as possible. Ralph said the work stoppages were occurring daily and Vance, being from outside the company, had neither the automotive experience nor the knowledge of Ford policy to deal with the situation. He was doing his best under the circumstances, but he was in an untenable situation.

Hunter told me there had been numerous discussions on how to address the labor situation, and the people at Ford felt it was time for a different perspective. He wished I could stay in Melbourne as there was more work to be done in the Asia Pacific region, but he understood the company did not have the luxury in New Zealand for on-the-job training with another Ford industrial relations director. I knew more about New Zealand labor relations than anyone in the company, and Ford needed to address the labor issues as quickly as possible.

I had mixed emotions. On the one hand, I knew it would be a difficult job and I was reluctant to move the kids again. We liked Australia, but we knew our assignment there would end one day. On the plus side, it was an opportunity to oversee my own industrial relations department and report directly to the managing director. New Zealand had an excellent school system and was a great place to raise a family. The kids were still at an age where life revolved around Mom and Dad instead of friends and activities at school, so changing schools would not be difficult. Dorothy and I talked it over. I suggested to Dorothy that God had been preparing us for this move since April 1975 when we first talked about the feeling I had about leaving Australia. Selling our boat and caravan and our change in focus from Bermagui were all part of the plan God had for us. Dorothy agreed, excited to see what God had in store for us in New Zealand. The next day, I let Hunter know we would accept the move, and the wheels were set in motion for us to go to New Zealand as soon as visas could be obtained.

We made our last trip to Bermagui in October to say goodbye to Johnny, Phil, Shirley, Cindy, and a few other friends.

They held a farewell party for us with lots of good food, drink, laughter, and yes, a few tears. I believe God brings people into our life for a purpose, and I felt blessed to have known these down-to-earth folks. I thanked the Lord for the kindness they brought into our lives. Johnny and Phil gave me an appreciation of a much simpler life where money was important but not high on their list of priorities. Enjoying each day and what it had to offer was more important as was family, friends, and a job—in that order—and, of course, a beer at the pub. As Johnny used to say, "People are more important than things." I was always quick to remind Johnny and Phil not to leave God out of the discussion. "In the end, your relationship with Christ is all that really matters."

Moving would be simpler this time as there was no furniture to move. Dorothy and the kids would stay in Melbourne until school ended in December. Hopefully by then I would have found a place to live, and this would cut down on our time in a hotel. I let Mom know of our relocation, and when I told her to start planning a trip to New Zealand, she just laughed. Ron and Ina were not surprised and hoped they could visit also. There were several going-away parties with co-workers and friends in Melbourne. At the company party, I contemplated the difference in saying goodbye to Ford co-workers and personal friends. Saying goodbye to co-workers was more of a celebration of a job well done as part of the Ford family, like saying, "No need to thank me. It was part of my job. We'll meet up again." Parting with friends like Johnny and Phil Cudd was leaving something behind—a bond of friendship we both chose to nourish and build upon.

The Lord had richly blessed our time Down Under.

# CHAPTER 7: EVERYONE LOVES NEW ZEALAND

*"But the wisdom that comes from heaven is first of all pure; then peace-loving, considerate, submissive, full of mercy and good fruit, impartial and sincere." James 3:17*

*(left to right) Dorothy, Dennis, Luanne, and Dennis in South Island, New Zealand, 1977.*

All international flights to New Zealand, such as my flight from Sydney, land first in Auckland, which has much longer runways and is suited to receive larger planes than Wellington. Then, passengers are connected by local flights to their destinations.

The DC-8 I was riding into Wellington was buffeted by strong and gusty winds as the plane made its final approach to the airport on November 1, 1975. I tightened my seat belt. I have never landed on an aircraft carrier, but I imagine it would be like landing in Wellington. The runway is short by commercial standards—approximately 6,000 feet—and the channeling effect of the Cook Strait frequently creates rough and turbulent winds. Wellington is the windiest city in the world with an average wind speed of 20 mph.

Wellington, the capital of New Zealand, had approximately 250,000 residents in 1975. The city is located at the southern tip of the North Island, between the Cook Strait and the Rimutaka Range. The temperature is moderate with an average of sixty-five degrees Fahrenheit in the summer and fifty degrees in the winter.

Ralph Fawcett, managing director of Ford New Zealand, and Hunter Pickens had already talked to Vance about my replacing him. He was disappointed, but he accepted the realty of the situation. Vance and I had spent time together on a previous trip of mine to New Zealand and numerous hours on the telephone, so we knew each other quite well. I told Vance I was sorry his tenure as industrial relations director had not worked out. He thanked me and confessed the job was emotionally draining. With no end in sight to the labor problems, he was keen to move on and grateful to Ford for the severance package. He already had several jobs offers he was considering. Vance and I kept in touch for a year or so after his departure and remained friends.

I found a beautiful three-bedroom house in the suburb of Khandallah overlooking Wellington Harbor. The house, built on a cliff about 1,000 feet above the strait, offered a picture-postcard view of the city and harbor. How fortunate to find such a house to lease my first week in Wellington! The house, a single-story white brick, had been totally remodeled and was ready to move into.

One of our first priorities after arriving in New Zealand was finding a church home. We were fortunate to find a Presbyterian

Church that we attended during our time in Wellinton. It was a little more dogmatic than other churches we attended, but we loved the people we met.

New Zealand is beautiful—tropical like Hawaii in the north and temperate like Norway in the south where there are also mountains and fiords. If you like the outdoors—hiking, fishing, sailing, or playing rugby, it is the place to live. World-class sailors come from New Zealand and have skippered on several America's Cup yachts. The All Blacks have dominated international rugby competitions for years and are the team to beat. The country is egalitarian with many subsidized social programs such as education, agriculture, housing, and medicine. In return, the taxation rate is extremely high, forty percent and up on annual income for most people. Unfortunately, a high percent of the brightest New Zealanders leave for Canada, Europe, and the US to further their careers and avoid the high taxation. Taxes on my income earned in New Zealand were offset against my US income tax, so I was reimbursed by Ford for taxes paid above the US tax rate.

## PRINCIPLE 3: PERSPECTIVE.

Perspective is the way you look at or view something. See things through God's perspective. Colossians 3: 1–3, "Since, then, you have been raised with Christ, set your hearts on things above, where Christ is, seated at the right hand of God. Set your minds on things above, not on earthly things. For you died, and your life is now hidden with Christ in God." Philippians 4:9, "Whatever you have learned or received or heard from me, or seen in me—put it into practice. And the God of peace will be with you." As we read in the Lord's Prayer (Matthew 6:10), Christ brought God's Kingdom to earth, for us to put into practice, "your kingdom come, your will be done, on earth as it is in heaven."

Perspective may change as you gain knowledge or look at subject matter from different angles. Oswald Chambers wrote,

"Seeing is never believing: we interpret what we see in the light of what we believe." This is also true for Christians. As we mature in our walk with Christ, our perspective changes. First Corinthians 13:12, "For now we see only a reflection as in a mirror; then we shall see face to face. Now I know in part; then I shall know fully, even as I am fully known." In Romans chapters 14 and 15, the Apostle Paul instructs Christians not to be judgmental or critical of one another based on disputable matters. Paul is more concerned about how we deal with differences than about the fact that we have differences. Christ does not require us to agree on every issue, but he does call us to love one another.

Worldly influence makes it increasingly difficult to see events solely through God's eyes. As Christians it is essential that we are guided by the inspired Word of God and the Holy Spirit. Do not confuse what you believe about God with believing in God. Christianity is a personal relationship with Jesus not a doctrine.

As witnesses for Christ, the more we understand why others believe what they believe the more effective we will be in sharing the gospel, resolving conflict, and building relationships.

As a former negotiator, I can attest biblical principles work well in all aspects of life. A statement establishes facts or views while asking questions elicits information. When discussing beliefs with people, the difference is relational—being engaged with others. Do you want an audience or a relationship? Make it a practice to get to know people; inquire about their well-being, family, and interests. Remove barriers, draw people closer to you, maintain a friendly demeanor, availability, and interest in others. As God's ambassadors, building relationships is key to making disciples or, for that matter, reaching satisfactory settlements with unions or government agencies.

New Zealand operates under a trade union system. Every trade had its own union. The largest and most militant of the six unions at Ford was the Coach Workers Union, chaired by Danny

Nichols. Danny had come to New Zealand from Liverpool, England, which in the 1960s had been a hot bed of union unrest. He was a union official in Liverpool during those turbulent times and was experienced in negotiating for more worker involvement in the English state-run industries.

New Zealand had been moving toward a socialist economic policy for the past several years. Unions were gaining strength under favorable labor laws. Many business leaders were concerned that New Zealand was following in England's footsteps. Reduction of the workforce had to be through redundancy, and temporary layoffs to accommodate production swings were not allowed. The definition of "health and safety" was so broad that work stoppages could be justified for almost any reason such as the quality of food in the cafeteria, unclean restrooms, and poor ventilation in the locker room. During stoppages, employees had to be paid up to twenty-four hours for time not worked. When a work stoppage lasted more than twenty-four hours, the first demand from the union to return to work was to pay the employees for the time they missed due to the work stoppage. During the late 1960s and the 1970s, New Zealand had the largest number of industrial disputes in its history, which trended the rate of labor disputes in England.

Shortly after arriving on the job, I arranged a meeting with Danny Nichols and the five other union leaders. Danny was short, maybe 5 foot, 5 inches, and 140–150 pounds. He had dark brown hair, wore thick eyeglasses, was clean-shaven, and dressed in denim pants and a flannel shirt, buttoned at the top. I introduced myself to each of the six trade union leaders in the Lower Hutt plant with a handshake. To my surprise, Danny said they already knew who I was, when I had arrived in Wellington, and why I had come to replace Vance Hainsworth. I said I sincerely hoped we could turn a new page and resolve future issues by negotiation instead of work stoppages. My door was always open, I insisted, and I was available to discuss issues at any time. I had worked with unions in many different countries, I added, and had a reputation of being fair and open minded.

After I finished my speech, Danny politely responded in his Liverpool accent that he appreciated my words but the goal of the unions was to have a voice in how the company was run and eventually have ownership in the company. The unions did not accept the idea of multi-national companies like Ford Motor Company operating in New Zealand under foreign ownership. I did not know whether to laugh or cry. So much for my conciliatory remarks! My first thought was he must be joking, yet I knew Danny was serious. Vance Hainsworth could attest to that. There was little input from the other union leaders during this discussion; it was obvious that Danny was in charge and was very competent.

"In that case," I politely said to Danny with a smile, "we have a lot to talk about, so let us keep it friendly." On this aggressive note, I started my relationship with Danny and the Coach Workers Union.

A major area of contention with the union was production schedules. A work standard is calculated by the time required by an average skilled operator, operating at a normal pace, to perform a specific task using a prescribed method. The use of work standards is a recognized practice throughout the automobile industry—and elsewhere—to determine fair production quotas. Occasionally, Ford negotiated with a union over the content of a job but never on the company's right to establish and enforce a work standard itself. Every time an industrial engineer attempted to time a new function to evaluate the efficiency of the process and to create accountability criteria, the workers stopped.

The Ford staff and the unions slowly made progress resolving plant-related issues, but we were at a standstill on management rights including work standards. Management rights basically determined who would run the company.

Early in 1976, I submitted a petition to the New Zealand Minister of Labor asking if he would appoint a mediator to review the management rights issues between Ford Motor Company and the unions. I invited Danny to participate in the discussions which he refused, stating that the union already had the right to not negotiate work standards or anything else they felt were already their rights.

When the final Ministry of Labor report was issued in August 1976, it vindicated Ford's position on management rights and provided Ford the framework needed to confidently proceed when negotiating with the unions in the future.

There were two key items recommended in the mediator's report. First, apart from legitimate health and safety issues, there was a call for a three day "cooling off period" with mediation before a strike could be authorized. If the unions engaged in unauthorized work stoppages during the mediation period, the workers would not be paid for their time. Secondly, decisions regarding work standards, production schedules, hours of work, and similar processes were affirmed as management issues that were the prerogative of Ford New Zealand and not of the unions. While the report did not carry the force of the law, it provided the basis for the Labor Ministry to issue regulations and recommend changes to the labor law if the parties did not comply. While the mediator's report applied specifically to Ford, it set the standard for the entire auto industry.

The unions initially rejected the recommendations of the mediator, but with the threat of more stringent controls from the Labor Ministry, they began to comply. Change did not happen overnight; we still suffered work stoppages and disruptions in the plant, but we were moving in the right direction. By the end of 1976, work stoppages were reduced from daily to three or four times a month. We also initiated work standards based on time studies and held weekly meetings with the union to address potential labor issues before they occurred. By 1977 the labor situation had stabilized in Lower Hutt. The previous two years had been difficult, but the progress was evident.

New Zealand's South Island is noted for its beauty—mountains, glaciers, and fjords. Eager to enjoy its beauties, Dorothy, the kids, and I made a two-week tour by automobile around the South Island in April 1976. Commercial car ferries run daily from Wellington to Picton on the north coast of the South Island. The sixty-mile trip across the Cook Strait normally takes about three hours and occasionally can get rough enough to warrant canceling the crossing. Picton was a quaint little seaport with a population of about 2,800 residents. We loved Picton and the surrounding harbor from the moment we saw it. As we got to know the area better, we realized the potential for boating in the Marlborough Sounds—miles of isolated water interspersed with islands and inlets extending south along the coast.

The following year, May 1977, I had the pleasure of fishing at Lake Taupo on the North Island, 230 miles north of Wellington. The lake, the largest freshwater lake in New Zealand, and its numerous tributaries provide some of the best rainbow and brown trout fishing in the world. Dorothy, Luanne, Dennis, and I stayed at Huka Lodge near Lake Taupo. Located on the Waikato River and surrounded by snow-capped mountain peaks and lush wilderness, Huka Lodge was a premier resort specializing in fly fishing.

In early 1978, on a trip to the northern shore of the South Island, we found an old wooden-hull boat set on blocks at the Picton Marina. I said to Dorothy that the boat looked sad and needed a new owner who would take care of her. (I suspect Dorothy saw what was coming!) Twenty-eight foot long with a single inboard engine, the boat needed some paint and maintenance, but it had four bunks, a small head, and a galley, ideal for cruising in the Marlborough Sounds. We bought the boat and contracted with the marina to paint it, to effect general clean up, and to service the motor. As soon as our new/old boat was ready in February 1978, we started an on-going nautical adventure we will never forget.

You need to be self-sufficient and have adequate supplies if you are to cruise safely in the Sounds. There was limited radio contact due to the mountainous terrain. Each trip, we would explore a new area and venture farther from Picton. In the afternoon, we anchored in a protected cove, caught fish for dinner, went swimming or hiking on the islands, and, sometimes, we just relaxed.

When Henry Ford II, Edsel Ford, and Philip Caldwell came to visit Ford New Zealand in 1978, Dorothy and I had the pleasure of spending time with them. Mr. Ford joked how each time he went to a different country, he would run into us. Dorothy and Edsel Ford spent the evening talking golf. Edsel said, if time had permitted, he would have played a round of golf at the Lower Hutt Country Club with Dorothy.

In November, Hunter Pickens called and said Philco-Ford Brazil wanted to talk to me about the position of director of industrial relations. Ford had purchased Philco in early 1961 and created Philco-Ford Brazil shortly thereafter. This was a larger, more diverse operation than any I had worked at before. Being director of industrial relations was clearly a promotion, and I was totally taken aback. Hunter suggested I talk to Dorothy and let him know in a few days as Philco was anxious to fill the position.

I could not see much wrong with a higher salary, and I knew I had completed my work as the New Zealand labor situation was stabilized with few disputes from the unions. In addition, George Hicks, my labor relations manager, had demonstrated that he could replace me as industrial relations director, and I could be of more use to Ford elsewhere. It was a good time to take on new challenges. Hunter said I had been specifically requested by Ed Launberg, managing director of Philco-Ford Brazil. My previous assignments were at Ford locations in transition or in startup mode, and this one would be no different. Philco-Ford Brazil was in the process of significant changes in its organization and business model. I guess you could say I was like an itinerant minister moving about helping improve existing operations or starting new ones.

Hunter then told me something I had not expected to hear. He said I was highly regarded by management in Dearborn and I had a reputation of accepting and completing difficult assignments whenever and wherever requested by the company. They liked the enthusiasm I exhibited by accepting these assignments based on company need rather than based on furthering my career. Too often, criteria such as promotion, salary increase, and career development are the only basis for management employees accepting an assignment. Hunter understood I never based my success on career goals. My abiding goal was to give one hundred and ten percent to my job and to be a good Christian witness wherever I went. God would take care of the rest.

"Having friends like you doesn't hurt either," I quipped. Hunter just laughed.

I talked to Dorothy that night, and she cried. We had become so attached to New Zealand and personal friends that the thought of leaving was painful. In the end, we did what we always did: we prayed about it. The Lord had never let us down, and we knew it would be no different this time.

Seeing how difficult it was for Dorothy to move again made me question if accepting the position was the right decision for my family. For me, the culture and the work environment in Ford was familiar no matter the country or the location; I often knew or was acquainted with employees in a new Ford location. For Dorothy, the transition to a new assignment was not as simple. She would have to cope with the day-to-day of living in a new culture, learning where to shop, how to navigate a new language and customs, and most importantly, making new friends and guiding Luanne and Dennis to new friendships in a new school. We would be starting all over again. When I told Dorothy of my concern, she would not hear of it.

"We are in this together," she replied. "We are where God wants us to be." End of discussion.

In the end, the decision proved simple. I had completed my assignment in New Zealand, Ford had opened another opportunity for us in Brazil, and there was no logical reason not to accept the promotion unless we wanted to go back to the US to finish my career. We followed our "Open Door Policy": when the Lord opened a door for us, we walked through it. At the time, I was unaware of the impact the move to Philco-Ford Brazil would have on my future career. Philco-Ford Brazil was part of the non-automotive Diversified Product Operations that I previously had little contact with, but that was about to change. The next day, I let Hunter know we were interested in taking the position.

I flew to Dearborn on November 26, 1978, to interview with Edwardo Launberg who had been appointed managing director of Philco-Ford Brazil. Brazilian by birth and education, he had earned a bachelor's degree in electrical and electronics engineering and an MBA in finance. Though Brazilian, Ed had European ancestry, spoke fluent English, was about six foot with short black hair, and was neatly attired in a dark blue suit and yellow tie. Ed and I met over lunch and began to get to know each other as he described the current state of the business in Brazil. Ed was in the process of launching several new products and building a new television manufacturing plant in Manaus on the Amazon River 1,672 miles north of Sao Paulo.

It was apparent Ed Launberg had prepared for our interview. He knew of my work in Venezuela, Australia, and New Zealand and felt I was the perfect candidate for industrial relations director. Following lunch, Ed offered me the position and said he looked forward to having me on his team. I was impressed with his friendly but straightforward manner and readily accepted the offer. We agreed to a January 1979 arrival in Sao Paulo.

I spent the next four days at the Ford World Headquarters getting acquainted with Philco-Ford Brazil and deciding which furniture to ship to Brazil from storage in Dearborn. I had dinner with Mom and Ron and Ina to inform them of our impending move to Brazil. We discussed the possibility we could remain with international operations until retirement. Of course, Mom and Ron and Ina preferred we come home but understood the ministry God had provided Dorothy and me at Ford. If God wanted us back home, doors would open for that to happen. Before returning to New Zealand, Ford provided a Berlitz Portuguese course that provided cassette tapes I could listen to on a small recorder that I took everywhere with me. I was a little rusty with my Spanish but pleasantly surprised at how quickly I picked up Portuguese.

During my last week in the office, while I was cleaning out some things, there was a knock on the door and Danny Nichols walked in. I smiled and asked him to sit down. He said he was concerned as to who would replace me. I told him it would be a US foreign service employee, but I felt confident that George Hicks, as the interim labor relations director, would make sure that operations would go smoothly in the plant.

Danny looked at me intently and then he said he was thinking of retiring from the union and the company.

"Why would you want to do that?" I asked.

"It took me two years," he replied, "to break you in, and I don't want to start over again."

We both laughed.

"We had our differences, Danny," I said, "but I never took it personally."

"I agree," he replied and extended his hand. We both said, "Goodbye and best of luck."

He turned and left the office. As the door shut behind him, I could not help but think how God had used Danny to teach me about Perspective and Patience. I later heard that Danny retired the following year and remained in Wellington with his family.

# CHAPTER 8: ON TO BRAZIL

*"In their hearts humans plan their course,*
*but the Lord establishes their steps."*
Proverbs 16:9

*(left to right) Dennis, Dorothy, Luanne, and*
*Dennis on a cruise in Rio, Brazil, 1981.*

Dorothy, Luanne, Dennis, and I returned from New Zealand to Dearborn in time for Christmas 1978 and moved into a company apartment. Ron, Ina, John, Rhonda, and Charlynn were now living in Traverse City, Michigan. Taking Mom with us, we spent Christmas together at their home in Traverse City. The kids had a great time sledding with their cousins and making a snowman, which was a new experience for Luanne and Dennis.

My first trip to Brazil was on January 7, 1979. Dorothy and the kids stayed in Dearborn until I could find a house in Sao Paulo. Looking from the Varig 747 aircraft window on our approach to Guarulhos International Airport, I could see the city of Sao Paulo was immense in size, the largest in Brazil and eleventh largest in the world with approximately twelve million people. Driving in the city can dull the senses of even the most patient of drivers—horns blaring, bumper to bumper traffic interspersed with bicycles, and motor scooters darting through traffic like bees buzzing around a beehive. Sao Paulo is a city of contrasts, a melting pot of many nationalities and cultures, the largest GDP in South America and eleventh largest in the world, yet infrastructure, pollution, and poverty are problems throughout the region. As Dorothy and I would soon learn, the people are industrious, friendly, and above all, fun loving.

The next morning, a company driver took me to the Philco-Ford Brazil headquarters. Philco, a manufacturer of consumer electronics and world-wide satellite tracking systems, was acquired by Ford in 1961 along with the Ford Aerospace and Communications Corporation. At the time I had no idea how significantly FACC would play in my future.

The current industrial relations director, Roberto Rela, age sixty-five, had been with the company for almost twenty years and was ready to retire. He had agreed to stay on for a few months after my arrival to ensure a smooth transition.

One of the benefits of being a director was a company car and a driver. Having a driver was a big help during the first several months as I got to know my way around in the hectic traffic and for Dorothy to run errands while settling into our house.

Sao Paulo, twenty degrees latitude closer to the equator than Wellington, was more tropical with an average high of seventy-five degrees Fahrenheit versus sixty-six degrees in Wellington. Labor and union issues were almost non-existent, with both the company and union focused on growing the company and improving the lives of the workforce through training and development. I had a good team reporting to me which allowed for more time to focus on building a new television manufacturing plant in Manaus.

One of the promises I had made to the kids when coming to Brazil was they could have a dog. Shortly after arriving in Sao Paulo, I bought a ten-week-old female black Labrador puppy. I was still living in the hotel at the time and would sneak the pup into the room under my coat at night. I also gave the maid a few extra *cruzeiros* to not turn me in! Our new house was still being remodeled, but it had a kennel where the puppy could stay. In the morning, I would drop the puppy off at the house. Then at midday, I'd drive the half hour from the office to feed her. When Luanne and Dennis saw the little Labrador puppy, they were so excited. They named her Abby. That was just the beginning of our animal menagerie. During our time in Brazil, the kids had rabbits, turtles, cats, guinea pigs, and parrots.

Soon after their arrival, I took Dorothy and the kids to Rio for Carnival. The Brazilian Mardi Gras was an annual five-day event beginning the Friday before Ash Wednesday. You must see the parade to believe it—an estimated one million spectators along the two-mile parade route! From our seats high in the grandstand overlooking the parade route, you could see several city blocks in each direction: choreographed dances from Samba schools, floats, marching bands, fancy costumes, revelers, you name it. The parade officially started at eight p.m. and was still going strong when we left at two a.m. to walk back to the hotel. It was one big party wherever you went in the country.

Dorothy decided it would be best to have a maid due to the size of the house. Maria was recommended to us by a friend. A Brazilian in her fifties, Maria had worked for expatriates before. She preferred not to live in as she had two school-aged children at home. Dorothy was fine with that as she liked to prepare the evening meal herself.

We attended the Calvary International Church located in Campo Bela, a suburb not far from home. Seventy percent of the 400-member congregation were expatriate families; the others were English-speaking nationals. Services were in English, but there was a strong outreach to the Brazilian community, and numerous English-speaking Brazilians were members of the church. Our pastor, Bill Fawcett, and his family had come to Sao Paulo as missionaries to the Portuguese-speaking community before pastoring at our church. For some Brazilian Christians, attending Calvary International was a way to improve their English and learn the gospel at the same time. Dorothy and I participated in mission outreach programs and hosted a Bible study on a regular basis. I inquired about New Tribes Mission and was told they had a base in the State of Amazonas, 1,200 miles to the north. I never attempted to contact them due to the distance, but New Tribes Mission will always have a special place in my memories. I still communicated with Jim Bou, but my ministry was now in Brazil.

Calvary International Church was our fourth church while living overseas. Not to diminish our pastors and friends at the other churches—we loved them all—but this was our favorite partly due to the mission outreach but mainly because of our involvement. The Bible study we had at our home grew to about twenty members over time. Not only did we share the love of Christ and scripture, but we also played on the same softball team and socialized together.

Luanne and Dennis went to an English-speaking international school operated by the US Embassy with financial support from the foreign and local business community. Dorothy drove the kids five miles to school most days; other days, the kids rode with friends' parents or would use my company driver. There were some Brazilian students in the international school who were preparing for college in the US. All students were required to take a class in Portuguese, which I thought was great.

It was rewarding and challenging to learn the consumer electronics business and its products. The new manufacturing plant in Manaus was my pet project. Philco-Ford Brazil company policies were like Ford corporate policies and had been revised to be commensurate with the electronics industry in Brazil. Due to the remote location of Manaus, we needed supplemental policies on compensation, recruitment, and training unique to that location.

As planned, Roberto Rela retired as industrial relations director in May 1979. I missed his advice on local issues, but he was only a phone call away if I needed him. Roberto was also the reason my Portuguese improved so rapidly as we always spoke in Portuguese, and he was quick to correct my pronunciation and grammar.

Of all my overseas assignments, Philco-Ford Brazil was my favorite from a work perspective. It was challenging to learn new technology and manufacturing processes, but the Brazilians are hard-working, fun-loving people. In-plant training was popular, and many employees took college courses after work. The company was financially stable and well run with competent management. There was some talk of Ford divesting itself from the consumer products business in the future, but nothing was imminent at the time.

Dorothy and I joined the Sao Paulo Golf Club located in Santo Amaro, six miles from our house. Ford paid the club dues for US foreign-service employees while the employee paid all additional costs: golf and locker room fees and meals. Dorothy, at her best on the golf course, won the women's championship two out of the four years she played there. Numerous professional US golfers played in tournaments hosted by the club, the most notable being Arnold Palmer in 1980. Dorothy had the pleasure of having lunch with Arnold and having a photo taken with him.

Once settled into our new life in Brazil, I began to explore fishing opportunities. Brazil was noted for its untapped freshwater fishing in the interior of the country. The same peacock bass we had caught in Venezuela were the primary game fish targeted by anglers. We sought many other species including the redtail catfish (up to fifty pounds) and the hard fighting golden dorado.

Dennis, now age twelve, and I made several fishing trips to remote locations. The one I remember most was a one-week trip with other expatriate friends from Sao Paulo and their sons to the Paraná River bordering on Paraguay. It was a long trip, but it was well worth the effort. We flew three hundred miles southwest from Sao Paulo to Curitiba and then had a six-hour trip by van on a two-lane bumpy road to the fishing lodge. One day, Dennis and I were fishing together in an eighteen-foot skiff and not getting bites. The day before we had caught fish in the same spot and wondered what had changed. We were about to move when something caught my eye in the maze of lily pads next to us. I said to Dennis, "Now I know why we aren't catching fish!" I pointed to a large alligator barely visible just twenty feet from the boat.

On another of our trips, we visited the Iguazu Falls, the largest waterfall system in the world. It is part of the Iguazu River which borders on Argentina. What a beautiful sight, much like Niagara Falls only three times larger.

Manaus had become famous for its rubber plantations in the early 1920s. By 1930, Manaus was called the Paris of the Amazon with its own opera house hosting world-famous musicians and singers. After world rubber markets collapsed in the late 1930s, however, Manaus became a ghost town. The world-famous opera house closed. There were intermittent power and water shortages, and sanitation systems deteriorated in the city. In the 1960s and 1970s, Manaus made a comeback when it became a government tax-free zone. The population grew from 400,000 in 1960 to approximately 600,000 by 1980. It was then that Philco-Ford Brazil, among other companies, began to move to the area. Located near the confluence of the Solimoes River and Rio Negro that form the Amazon River, Manaus was still a remote and isolated city, 1,000 miles inland from the Atlantic Ocean and accessed primarily by air or water.

It was difficult to find employees in Manaus. With new companies moving to the area, the demand for labor was greater than the supply. Most residents had minimal education, technical skills, or manufacturing work experience. We established a one-week training program for all new hires prior to starting employment. Once on the job, we continued training in manufacturing and technical skills. To shore up the work force, we encouraged Philco-Ford Brazil employees with technical and supervisory experience to leave Sao Paulo and transfer to Manaus. To make the move more attractive, we offered incentive packages for those who relocated. We also instituted temporary assignments for specialists to assist in the start-up so they would not have to make a long-term commitment. We hoped that some of these specialists might stay. Just in case, we also planned on developing a local force of specialists. We built low-cost housing and a medical facility near the plant to draw people to the area.

One of the highlights of our time in Brazil was in 1980 when Henry Ford II came on a farewell visit before his retirement. Len Halstead, president of Ford Brazil, held a farewell celebration at his house for Mr. Ford. Dorothy and I chatted with Mr. Ford about our previous meetings in Venezuela and New Zealand. He was a gracious man, easy to talk to and easy to laugh. Dorothy and other well-wishers are in pictures with Mr. Ford being presented with his retirement plaque.

The next year, Phil Caldwell, who replaced Mr. Ford as CEO, came to Sao Paulo to visit the Ford facilities. At a company dinner attended by all Ford management in Brazil, Mr. Caldwell remarked how Ford was a big family with members scattered around the world. He went on to say how pleased he was to see Dennis and Dorothy Blue again after just visiting with them in New Zealand the year before. I do not know about Dorothy, but I felt like standing and taking a bow.

One of the benefits of going to Manaus was the fishing. I made friends with some of the locals who would take me fishing on tributaries of the Rio Negro for peacock bass. The fishing was excellent, and being fluent in Portuguese made it possible for me to get to know the locals and their culture. I would sometimes spend the night in a small village outside Manaus enjoying local food such as *moqueca,* fish stew, and *feijoada,* black bean stew. They were humble people who lived off the land and were willing to share what they had. I would always bring gifts of food or other items they could use. Little did I know I would return to Manaus in the future as a fishing guide and translator.

In November 1981, almost three years after my arrival at Philco-Ford Brazil, the new plant in Manaus commenced operation with four hundred employees. Attending the inauguration along with Ed Launberg and local government dignitaries, I was proud to have been part of building a plant in the middle of the Amazon. This plant launch was reminiscent of the ones in Taiwan and the Philippines. While in Manaus, I also could not help but think of my time in Venezuela. In 1970, I was flying for New Tribes just five hundred miles northeast of where the plant now stood.

Shortly after returning to Sao Paulo, I received a call from Bill Gromer asking me when it would be convenient for him to come to Brazil to see the operations and talk to me about a move back to Dearborn. Bill was the executive assistant to Tom Page, executive vice president, Diversified Products Operations (DPO), reporting to Don Petersen, president and chief operation officer, Ford Motor Company. Mr. Page had responsibility for all ten non-automotive operations in the company including Philco-Ford Brazil.

Bill Gromer told me he was scheduled for a move the following spring, and Mr. Page had started a search for his replacement. Mr. Page had specifically asked Bill to talk to me as he felt my diverse background in overseas operations would fit well with the varied businesses that comprised DPO. I first met Mr. Page in 1976 in New Zealand when he was touring the Asia-Pacific Region. Neither he nor I will likely forget our first meeting. Dorothy and I invited him to our house for dinner one evening, and on that occasion, he spilled a glass of red wine on the carpet. He apologized and was obviously embarrassed. "No harm done," Dorothy said and cleaned up the wine stain. My second meeting with Mr. Page had been in Sao Paulo in 1980 when he was reviewing performance and long-term objectives at Philco-Ford Brazil.

Bill and I agreed he would come the following week.

That evening I filled Dorothy in on my conversation with Bill and the possibility of returning home. As she has done on so many previous occasions, Dorothy said, "Wherever God wants we will go. God has opened so many doors for us and has not let us down yet."

I thanked Bill for taking the time to come to Brazil and hoped it was not in vain. He laughed and said he would get back to me as soon as Mr. Page reached a decision.

The following week, I got a call from Bill saying Mr. Page would like to talk to me while I would be in Dearborn on home leave in December—which was only a month away. Dorothy and I talked about the possibility of returning home and agreed it was time. It would be good for Dennis and Luanne to move back into the US school system before high school and settle into the American way of life. Dorothy and I felt the children needed an American secondary education if they were to do well in an American college.

Where had the time gone? It had been almost fourteen years since we left home in 1968 for Venezuela. I was now almost fifty years old with one of the longest foreign-service tenures in the company. This could be our last chance to return home, further my career with Ford in the US, and get the kids into the American school system. Would God use Mr. Page to open the door to returning home?

Back in Michigan for the holidays, I met with Mr. Page on December 21, 1981, to discuss the position. The first half hour, we talked about family and how the company was doing. Only then did we talk about the position. He said he had been considering me as a replacement for Bill since his trip to Brazil the previous year, and if I wanted the job, it was mine. I was surprised at the quick offer and tried to appear casual in my reply. It did not work as I broke into a big smile and said, "When do you want me to start?" I then composed myself and sincerely said, "Mr. Page it would be my pleasure to work for you," and thanked him for giving me his confidence.

"No need to thank anyone," Mr. Page said. "You have earned your promotion."

*Yes, I do. Thank you, Lord,* I said to myself. "Mr. Page, you may not know it, but God has used you to open another door for us." I smiled and thought to myself, "When Dorothy and I made the difficult decision to leave New Zealand for the unknown world of Philco-Ford Brazil and Diversified Products Operations, it was a step of faith. Now I know why we were led there!

Ron, Ina, and Mom were happy we were coming home, but each of them said they would believe it when they saw it. We spent Christmas with Mom in her apartment in Riverview and then drove north to Traverse City to see Ron and Ina just before New Year's Eve. It was sort of a homecoming and New Year's celebration all in one.

The Christmas holiday was almost over, but before we returned to Sao Paulo, there was one piece of unfinished business. On December 27, I called a Tiara Yacht dealer in Gibraltar, a small town on Lake Erie only five miles from Grosse Ile where I had lived with my folks and had kept my boat in 1963. A person named Jim answered the phone, but he said they were closed for the holidays. I explained I had to return to Brazil right after the New Year and was hoping to see what they had in stock before I left. Jim said he would meet me at the dealership the next day. When I walked in, I thought I recognized the person sitting at the desk. I started to introduce myself and suddenly recognized it was Jim Diamond, an old buddy from my high school days. Jim recognized me about the same time and jumped up to give me a hug. We brought each other up to date on our lives over the past thirty years. Jim's dad had owned a restaurant in Flat Rock, and after he died, Jim and his brother Don took over the business. They eventually sold the restaurant, and Jim bought the Tiara dealership.

Now the real work of moving back home began. I contacted the renters of our house in Northville, which I had purchased as a real estate investment several years earlier, to advise them of our return. Fortunately, their lease expired at the end of May, so the timing was perfect for both them and us. I made a visit to the Country Day School, a private school in Birmingham, Michigan. Country Day was highly regarded academically because of its small classes and quality teachers. Luanne would be in the tenth grade and Dennis in the eighth grade. Neither had ever gone to school in the US, and we wanted to give them the best opportunity during the transition.

We returned to Sao Paulo on January 10, 1982, and began our countdown to departure. Most of our furniture would be sold before we left. Our Labradors, Abby and Buffy, would be sent to a dog kennel in Dearborn until we moved into our house. We effected change of address on numerous accounts and records and miscellaneous items to allow a smooth transition back into the US. The good news was we did not have to apply for a visa! The most difficult decision was what to do about Maria. We had similar feelings when we left our maid Esther behind in Venezuela. Maria was special. We had grown to love her as family, and it was difficult to leave her behind. She had one favor to ask. Could I get her son a job at Philco-Ford Brazil? "Of course," I replied as I gave her a big Brazilian "abrazo" hug.

When the day finally arrived for our departure in June 1982, we had mixed emotions. We were sad to leave our friends and home in Brazil but happy to return to life in the good old USA. What started out as a six-month assignment had come full circle fourteen years later. As we reflected on the many memories, the people we met, and the unforgettable experiences, we felt blessed that God had kept his hand on us during this chapter in our lives. There was more to come; God had another door to open for us.

# CHAPTER 9: BACK TO THE USA

*"And my God will meet all your needs according*
*to the riches of his glory in Christ Jesus."*
*Philippians 4:19*

*(left to right) Henry Ford II with cigar,*
*Lynn Halstead, president Ford Brazil with*
*plaque and Dorothy in blue and white stripe*
*dress in Brazil, 1980.*

When Dorothy, Luanne, Dennis, and I returned to the USA on June 14, 1982, we were coming to a home that we owned. This was different from our experience of the last fourteen years—essentially the only experience Luanne and Dennis knew.

We now had access not only to our own furniture and belongings, which had been in storage since our going to Venezuela in 1968, but we had John and Lucille's, which had also been stored following their deaths in 1969. It took a week of sorting through our collection of things we had not used in fourteen years to determine what we wanted to keep. Dorothy, the kids, and I spent a weekend selecting the major items such as furniture and personal belongings we could use in our new house. Mementos, which were easier to move out, were sorted during the day by Dorothy and the kids. When I would get home from work, we would talk about items she had found that brought back memories, some good and some difficult. She had a box for special treasures we wanted to remain with us. Some items—John and Lucille's being among them—we left in storage until we had more time to decide a final disposition; what we could not use we gave to the Salvation Army.

All was not "nose to the grindstone." The first weekend home, Dorothy, the kids, and I accepted delivery of our new thirty-one-foot Tiara which we named *True Blue*. Not to have the boat's "maiden voyage" postponed, I took Dorothy and the kids for a ride on Lake Erie. After introducing them to Jim Diamond, we set out on *True Blue*. It was everything I imagined; however, I could not have conceived what role *True Blue* would play in shaping my future.

Once again, the burden of setting up home life fell on Dorothy. She stayed on top of things while I was busy settling into my new job. I had accumulated vacation days, but it did not seem appropriate for me to take time off before reporting to an executive vice president. The way Dorothy pitched in reminded me (not that I had forgotten!) what a faithful and reliable partner she had been over the years. It would have been just about impossible for me to have a career overseas and raise a family without her support at home. Her immense contributions to our quality of life gave me a glimpse of the challenges for a single parent pursuing a career while raising a family and for families with both parents working. Having to depend on one another brought Dorothy, the kids, and me closer together as a family.

The first evening in our new home, Dorothy, Luanne, Dennis, and I gathered in prayer to thank God for watching over us and returning us home. What other doors would open in the future? We prayed we would be ready for whatever he had in store for us.

Interestingly, we had a period of adjustment settling back into the US. It was like another foreign assignment—well not quite, but the country and culture had changed since we left. Computers, cell phones, traffic, shopping malls—a lot can change in fourteen years. The kids adjusted to American school as they had never attended class in the US. It took time to get acquainted with the new system. They were ahead of their classmates in English and mathematics. They could name the capital of many countries around the world and their locations, but neither could name all the states in the US nor their capitals. Country Day School was the perfect place to make the transition as classes were small and the teachers excellent. During our years overseas, Luanne and Dennis had developed self-reliance and confidence as they moved to new schools and met new friends. Helping them to adjust was a family effort. Dorothy made sure she met the teachers and became involved in school activities. I checked on homework schedules and attended parent/teacher meetings. Together we all grew and benefited from the new experiences.

A big plus of returning was being close to Mom again. She was living in a senior-citizen apartment building about an hour from our house in Northville. We visited once a week, and she often came to stay with us. By December, things were back to normal, and we looked forward to our first Christmas in our own home in fourteen years. The concept of staying in the same home for more than a few years was new for us.

Tom Page, executive vice president of Diversified Products Operation (DPO), was responsible for all non-automotive operations in Ford and reported to Don Petersen, president, Ford Motor Company. Tom was a great person to work for. A delegator of authority, a visionary, and an innovator, he was a man ahead of his time in the corporate world. Tom believed in not only delegating responsibility but also empowering the delegates with the authority to do the job. He wanted everyone to feel they were a contributor, an asset to the company. Many of the organizational changes Ford would undergo in the future were initiated by Tom Page. We seldom scheduled a meeting during the workday. Instead, we met an hour or so after five p.m. to discuss important matters.

Ford and the automotive industry were moving from vertical integration to outsourcing. DPO—comprised of ten diverse non-automotive businesses with products ranging from steel to casting, plastics, glass, tractors, electronics, climate control, aerospace, microelectronics, and consumer electronics—would all be dramatically impacted by the coming changes. Tom confided that his primary reason for wanting me was my diverse experience in overseas operations where I had been instrumental in resolving conflicts and getting parties to agree on outcomes. He felt I had the background he needed to help him on this DPO restructuring plan which promised to "ruffle many feathers." He was looking to me to help make the transitions outlined in those plans as painless as possible for all employees involved.

Nancy Bedow, who reported to me, had been a colleague of Tom Peters, the guru of organizational management and the author of the best-seller *In Search of Excellence*. Nancy would focus on the reorganization of DPO and make recommendations to Tom Page and me. Nancy and I held several meetings with Tom Peters to develop processes that could be used by management in downsizing and integrating operations within DPO.

I also was involved in maintaining regular DPO administrative work as we were still a functioning part of Ford. My role as executive assistant, Industrial Relations DPO, was to oversee human resources for the ten divisions that reported to Tom Page. The most interesting part of my job was acquiring insight into how executive decisions were made at the top of the company. Working for an executive vice president also meant I was involved in meetings where corporate decisions were made. On numerous occasions in my after-hours meetings with Tom, executives such as Philip Caldwell, chief executive officer, and Don Petersen, president, would walk in unannounced and talk business. Tom was well respected, and his opinion valued by top management. Mr. Caldwell was gracious enough to signal we knew each other. He recalled our meeting both in New Zealand and in Brazil, and his acknowledgement made me feel part of the team.

It did not take long for information about a restructuring of DPO to emerge in the divisions. With Tom Page's permission, I held a meeting with the DPO division industrial relations managers to bring them up to date. Nancy Bedow and I explained the need and the philosophy of the restructuring and divestitures that were being considered. We stressed that nothing had been decided yet. These changes were no surprise to most of the divisions; they were already aware of the increasing competition from automotive-component suppliers outside of Ford and the need for Ford to focus on its core automotive business. Nancy and I assured the industrial relations managers they were a key part of a successful transition and we would keep them informed as plans were developed. Everyone was appreciative of our transparency, and our open strategy created an atmosphere of cooperation that served DPO and the divisions well during those difficult transition times. Looking back, that meeting was providential. I doubt if my yet-unknown future role in the DPO transition would have been successful without the mutual trust established with the division industrial relations managers in that meeting.

Jack Hall, my counterpart as the industrial relations director for the North American Automotive Operation [NAAO] was a big help and supporter. He reported to Harold "Red" Poling, executive vice president of NAAO. Mr. Poling would one day become CEO of Ford Motor Company. Organizationally, Red Poling was responsible for automotive operations, and Tom Page for non-automotive operations. Jack and I understood that NAAO would be the core of Ford's future business while DPO would decline and eventually phase out. It was important that we worked together to ensure a smooth transition from DPO to outside suppliers and to accommodate displaced DPO personnel within the automotive operations. At the same time, we needed to "flatten" the Ford organization structure and eliminate levels of management and tiers of unnecessary reporting. Jack and I organized an offsite weekend seminar with all DPO and NAAO industrial relations managers to address organizational changes and encourage cooperation between divisions. It was a big success as it broke down barriers between divisions that had existed for years. Jack Hall was always glad to share information with me. We became good friends and kept in touch after retirement.

By 2000, seven of the DPO operations had been sold to outside buyers and the remaining operations (climate control, electronics, and interior systems) were spun off to the newly created Visteon Corporation, which was separated from Ford. Of the approximately 20,000 employees affected, ninety percent were placed in Ford or the new companies. Some took early retirements or separation pay, and others we assisted in placement outside of Ford.

Things were good on the home front. In 1983, Dorothy and I joined the Washtenaw Golf Club in Ypsilanti so Dorothy could play golf. She was the club champion for five years in a row. I was glad to see her enjoying her new life in the US as she had earned it!

Salmon were introduced to Lake Michigan, Lake Ontario, and Lake Huron in the 1950s, and these lakes quickly developed into a world-class sport fishery. We liked Humbug Marina, where we kept *True Blue*, but there were no salmon in Lake Erie where the marina was located. The kids and I wanted to try salmon fishing, so in 1983, we moved the boat to Betsie Bay Marina in Frankfort, Michigan, one of the premier salmon fishing ports on Lake Michigan. Despite the two-hundred-mile trip from Northville, we headed to Frankfort every weekend, and the boat became our summer cottage. Fishing was great! We caught twenty-pound chinook salmon almost every outing.

We liked much about Frankfort. The fishing and friends were great, but the boat traffic on weekends was challenging. One Saturday morning, I counted two hundred fishing boats within sight. The following week, I decided to explore the less-busy port of Onekama, located on Portage Lake with access to Lake Michigan. When I talked to Jim Mrozinski, owner and manager of Onekama Marine, a family-owned marine facility providing new boat sales, service, storage, and two marinas on Portage Lake, I felt convinced making a move was the right choice. Jim was polite, yet businesslike, a large man in his forties with a mariner's hat. His parents, Walter and Clara, had started Onekama Marine in 1963, and Jim grew up working at the marina. You could tell it was a way of life for him as the marina reflected his passion.

We booked winter storage at Onekama Marine for 1983 and a slip in the marina for the spring of 1984, which I retained until 2016 when I sold my boat. I became a stockholder and board member of the marina in 1987.

One of our early tasks was to find a church home. We settled on the United Methodist Church in Northville where we had friends that I knew from Ford. One day, Pastor Eric Hammer would marry our daughter Luanne in that church.

In the fall of 1984, we enrolled in a Bible study held one night a week. It was taught by one of the Sunday school teachers from the church. There were thirty adults in the class—some were church members and others came from outside the congregation. Following completion of the four-week Bible study, we asked four couples we had met during the class—Dale and Sherry Krugel, Ron

110

and Linda Frederick, Jim and Karen Bonnell, and Greg and Sharon Rhodes—if they would like to continue a one-hour Bible study each Tuesday at our house. None of the couples were members of our church, but they were interested in learning more about the Bible. I told them our study is not about doctrine but a personal relationship with Jesus Christ. They were excited to participate.

During our time together, we became close friends. Dorothy and I invited them for weekends at our condo in Onekama where we enjoyed fishing and skiing together. Three of the couples had children, and I think our kids enjoyed the social aspect even more than the adults.

We continued to meet in 1985 for a second year of Bible study; Dorothy and I had requests from others at church to join us. Since we did not have the room, a second group formed in another home.

After our last session of studying Revelation for six weeks, I asked Sherry Krugel if she would write a synopsis of our study. She hesitated but then agreed. Two weeks later, Sherry made her presentation to the group. Revelation is not an easy book of the Bible to understand. Final judgement (eschatology) and the end times (apocalypse) are difficult even for scholars. Inspired by the Holy Spirit, Sherry presented a clear, precise, and biblically-sound synopsis of Revelation. We were blessed because we all grew as Christians and stayed friends over the years as brothers and sisters in Christ. In 2002, three of the four original couples met in Florida for a reunion.

In 1985, I began to study for my United States Coast Guard Captain's License—just in case I might need it one day. I completed the course the following year and officially received my license in the spring of 1986. The thought of having a charter business one day continued to be intriguing. Even if I never used the captain's license commercially, it has made me a better seaman.

In early 1985, Tom Page retired at age sixty-seven, the mandatory retirement age at Ford. It was a pleasure working for him. Tom was a gentleman, and I was sorry to see him leave. He was replaced by Phil Benton, vice president sales and marketing for Ford. Phil was a high-energy person, extremely bright, who went on to become president of Ford Motor Company.

# CHAPTER 10: TRANSITIONING TO RETIREMENT

*"And we know that in all things God works for
the good of those who love him, who have been
called according to his purpose." Romans 8:28*

*Arnold Palmer and Dorothy in Sao Paulo, 1980.*

Following Tom Page's retirement, I entered the last phase of
my career with Ford, but I did not know it then. It was only as the
months and the special assignments ensued that I came to formulate
and enact a plan for my exit.

In 1985, DPO began to implement our restructuring plan to
divest or outsource non-automotive business. The divestiture would
be long and complicated, and it would not be finalized until 2000. I
had been involved in the early planning with Tom Page before his

retirement and was to be deeply involved in the beginning stages of implementation.

In August 1986, Phil Benton asked me to serve on a four-person task force reporting to Pete Pestillo, vice president industrial relations for Ford, to study employee and organizational practices in other corporations to inform our DPO restructuring. Mr. Pestillo felt it was important to have a non-automotive perspective on this task force, and he specifically requested me to fill that capacity.

After we convened, the task force chose to study Dupont, Boeing, Hewlett Packard, TRW, General Electric, and the Stanford School of Business. What a unique experience to observe firsthand some of the country's most successful organizations. We travelled extensively to their headquarters located from Connecticut to California. We spent several days at each business or school as we met with key management to exchange ideas and learn their best practices.

We made a final report to Ford corporate management in December 1986 stating the ten best employee and organizational practices to guide Ford. The report was enthusiastically accepted and became part of the restructuring plan that Ford was undertaking. A copy of the final report was given to each of the participating companies, and each member of the task force received a special commendation from Pete Pestillo for a job well done. It did not look bad on our resumes either!

I returned to DPO in January 1987 after my interesting assignment on the task force. Ed Williams had replaced Phil Benton as vice president of DPO, and Phil had been promoted to president of North American Operations. Because of my experience with the task force, I was made responsible for restructuring and divestiture within DPO and given the title organization and special studies manager.

Ford Tractor, Philco-Ford Brazil, and Ford Aerospace and Communications Corporation were non-automotive businesses, and as such, they were first on the list to be considered for sale to buyers outside of Ford.

Ed Launberg was exploring potential buyers for the Philco-Ford operations in Brazil. I made several trips to Brazil in 1986 to assist Ed in employee benefits and compensation negotiations, but no agreements were reached. It had been four years since I left Brazil, but it seemed like yesterday. Most of the people I knew were still there, and we were glad to see each other. Sao Paulo seemed the same from the outside, but I was told the faltering economy in Brazil had increased poverty and crime in the city. It was troubling for me to discuss the sale of Philco-Ford Brazil with people I knew and worked with in Brazil. Many could be impacted by redundancy and by having to accept lower pay scales. I assured them we would do our best to protect employment and compensation for everyone, but only time would tell if we would be successful. Philco-Ford Brazil would eventually be sold, and I would be part of the negotiations.

Ford Aerospace and Communications Corporation had been spun off Philco-Ford in the 1960s and had become a successful space tracking and military defense subsidiary of Ford. It would be more complex to sell than Ford Tractor or Philco-Ford Brazil due to the numerous top-secret military contracts with the Department of Defense. Many of FACC employees were highly qualified technical people. There were concerns that some employees might leave rather than join the new ownership, and they would be difficult for the new owners to replace. In addition to the technical expertise, the company required numerous employees to qualify for security clearances to work on military contracts.

To add to these challenges, the vice president of industrial relations FACC, Neil Duff, retired unexpectedly in October 1986 due to health problems. Unfortunately, there was no one in FACC qualified to replace him. Finding a qualified replacement from inside Ford itself would not prove easy because it was not an advantageous transfer. Ford had a policy requiring that a Ford

115

employee transferring to a subsidiary be placed on the subsidiary payroll and governed by their compensation and benefit policies. Generally, Ford benefits were superior to those of subsidiaries, and so the subsidiaries were not attractive as a transfer. Several Ford employees were qualified to replace Neil, but during interviews for the FACC position, they learned they would have to leave the Ford payroll and the more lucrative Ford compensation and benefits packages. Transfer to a subsidiary that not only had lower benefits but was up for sale offered only chancy long-term prospects. Understandably, they all declined rather than sign on for lower benefits and an uncertain future with a new owner. As a result, there was no one both qualified and willing to replace Neil Duff from within Ford.

I began to wonder if I could take the position. It was possible to retire from Ford at fifty-five, but that early retirement carried with it a fifty percent reduction in retirement benefits which was not an attractive option. However, the last three years had been difficult as I experienced the restructuring of DPO and saw how it could negatively affect people, some of them good friends. Contemplating this gave me pause to realize what I already believed, there was more to life than money. I began to think about what I wanted to do with the rest of my life.

I was in my prime earning years and in line for more bonuses and stock options. Why would I want to give up that security for something unknown? On the other hand, how much is enough? We had investments, and I would receive a pension—albeit reduced. At fifty-five, I would still have a lot of energy, and I could pursue a second career. I had been dreaming of becoming a charter captain for fishing expeditions since fishing in Australia. I talked to Dorothy about her expectation for the future, and as she has done over the years, she said, "Whatever you think is best is fine with me." Early retirement, if we took it, would be a major change in our lives; we would be leaving what we knew and enjoyed for whatever uncertainty the future had to offer. We remembered, however, that our entire married life had been built on our faith and our trust in God for shaping the future. Again, we submitted to God. If the Lord wanted us to leave Ford, doors would be opened. If he did not, we would stay. We reminded ourselves of our efforts to leave Ford for Campus Crusade and Eastern Airlines in 1966, but doors were closed then, and we submitted. Then our great overseas adventure with Ford started in 1968. Something like that would happen again if it were meant to be.

John Slosar was in his early fifties, intelligent and charismatic, a warm and considerate person. He was a former star basketball player and a graduate of the University of Detroit. In March 1987, about four months after Neil Duff had retired, knowing the difficulty Ford was having in finding a replacement for him, I confided to John that if I could get assurance I could stay on the Ford payroll, I would take the position at FACC. When FACC was sold, I would take a special early retirement. He looked at me for a minute and said, "You are serious, aren't you?" I nodded yes and explained that I had decided it was time to see what the Lord had in store for Dorothy and me outside Ford. John and I had talked previously about my passion for fishing and having my own charter fishing business, so that part was no surprise to him, but my wanting to retire so soon did surprise him. He had graduated from a Jesuit school and remained close to his Catholic faith. Occasionally, he and I also talked about our faith, and he understood the strength of my faith journey.

I asked John to take the lead and talk to Ed Williams, vice president of DPO. If Ed agreed, we would request an exception to policy allowing me to stay on the Ford payroll and we would ask for an approval of a special early retirement. The "special" in early retirement was important as Ford could waive the reduction in the early retirement benefit. This waiver was reserved for employees under special circumstances such as the elimination of a position due to reorganization or a foreign-service employee returning to the US and finding no placement options in a commensurate position. We talked a while longer about logistics and the timing of the move. John felt the odds of approval were little to none. Ford has strictly adhered to the subsidiary transfer policy, and neither of us were aware of exceptions. At the time of John's and my discussion, Ford had already invested four months in searching for Neil Duff's replacement to no avail. The company still had no qualified candidates, and finding one was critical to proceeding with a sale of FACC. John said he would get back to me after discussing my proposal with Ed Williams.

Three days later, John came into my office and shut the door. Ed Williams liked the idea, as he was anxious to fill the position at FACC and start looking for a buyer. Craig Hausman, Ford director of personnel, approved an exception for me to remain on the Ford payroll and to receive a special early retirement. John talked to Don Rassier, president of FACC, who agreed in principle to hire me as vice president, industrial relations, FACC, but he wanted an interview with me before a final decision was made. I paused as I tried to take it all in.

"Everything was approved?" I asked when he was finished.

John took a breath and said, "I never thought it would be. You must have someone looking out for you."

"To be honest, neither did I, and yes, I do think Someone is looking out for me."

I thanked John Slosar for being a good advocate and hoped I could return the favor one day. I interviewed with Don Rassier a few days later, and he offered me the position. It was agreed I would start July 1, 1987, as vice president, industrial relations, FACC.

Of course, I had kept Dorothy informed of the progress of these discussions, but when I told her the breakthrough news that I was offered the position at FACC, she looked puzzled. "I thought

118

you said there was only one chance in a million you would move to FACC."

"I did think that." I replied. "That's what I thought, but with God all things are possible. That was one door only God could open."

We hugged, and as so many times in the past, we were excited about what God had in store for us now.

If I moved to FACC, I would require a top-secret security clearance as I would be dealing with classified information on military contracts for the Department of Defense. FACC, formerly part of Philco-Ford, had an impressive background in satellites and defense systems. In the 1960s, Philco-Ford had been a pioneer in the development and launch of aerospace tracking systems. They had built the original NASA Mission Control Center in Houston, Texas, and developed several air defense missile tracking systems. I do not believe it would be proper to go into the details even after thirty years, but knowing the tracking systems we had in place back then, it boggles my mind as to what must be available today.

Loral, a large defense contractor, was interested in acquiring FACC. As previously mentioned, many of the employees at FACC were highly educated professionals, aerospace engineers, scientists, physicists, and computer engineers with expertise that was highly sought after in the aerospace industry. As with negotiations at Philco-Ford Brazil, reconciling FACC and new-owner personnel policies, benefits, and compensation was critical to retaining key management and technical personnel. A trained and knowledgeable personnel is a main asset of the purchase of an existing company, so we were determined not to have a mass exodus due to unattractive features of the sale. I also worked on equitable relocation and severance polices for those employees made redundant by the sale. Ford wanted to ensure everyone was treated fairly.

One evening after most of the staff had left—it was about seven—I sat in my office looking out from the twenty-third floor.

119

The bright lights of Detroit and Windsor illuminating the waterfront of the Detroit River was magical. "How did I get here?" I pondered. It is a long way from a six-month assignment in Ford Venezuela to vice president, industrial relations, FACC. My first and correct answer was we had answered God's call whenever he opened a door for Dorothy and me, not because it was a career opportunity or promotion but because it served God's purpose. Scripture tells us in Romans 8:28, "And we know that in all things God works for the good of those who love him, who have been called according to his purpose." I believe that. I have seen it work in my own life. God led us back to Venezuela after the tragic death of Dorothy's parents. Our lives were forever changed as God guided us around the world with Ford to where I am now contemplating retirement and embarking on a new ministry. I have always viewed my work and position in life as ordained by God. He provides us with the gifts and opens the doors for us to fulfil his purpose no matter our station in life.

There were things God wanted me to accomplish and people who needed to hear about Christ's love for the lost. As we go through life, each of us is uniquely positioned to witness to someone no one else could reach. Working for a large corporation and travelling to other countries, we were fulfilling 2 Corinthians 5:20, "We are therefore Christ's ambassadors, as though God were making his appeal through us."

I am of the opinion witnessing in the workplace should be by word and deed not proselytizing. I do not think using your employer's time for other purposes is what God intended and often sends the wrong message to co-workers. Exhibiting Christian principles at work will be noticed by others. The Holy Spirit will provide the opportunity to talk about Jesus when the time is right. We must move away from the mindset that faith and work are in separate boxes in our lives.

One of the dilemmas Christians face in the workplace is which master do I serve, God or man. God's command to love our neighbor encompasses neighbors at our specific workplace. We should reject work practices that cause us to contradict God's word. Truthfulness, integrity, and kindness are respected principles sought by most employers no matter their religious beliefs. We should also respect our work: Colossians 3:23–24, "Whatever you do, work at it with all your heart, as working for the Lord, not for human masters, since you know that you will receive an inheritance from the Lord as a reward. It is the Lord Christ you are serving."

From a career perspective, staying with Ford for thirty years—my entire adult work life—provided continuity for a career path. A career is much like life: an accumulation of experiences. I had gone from the Ford management training program in Monroe, Michigan, to working for an executive vice president, DPO. I was at the high point of my career. Along the way, I honed innate skills and learned new ones that were not so intuitive. I accumulated knowledge, and here I was, thirty years later, about to retire and thinking how blessed I had been. I loved my work, gave one hundred and ten percent no matter the position, and the rewards followed.

I had a pleasant surprise when I received a letter forwarded from Ed Williams' office. Ed had written a note at the bottom. "Dennis, we are very proud of your work. Thanks, Ed." The letter written September 21, 1987, was from Don Rassier to Ed Williams. It was a complimentary report of my work at FACC and concluded, "Seldom has a person new to an organization been able to accomplish so much in less than three months, and I feel it appropriate to advise you of these results." I know it sounds like I am bragging, and truthfully, I am. It was hard work and long hours! But in the end, to God be the glory.

I never cease to be amazed at how the Lord works things out. To the skeptic, I know it may be explainable as the course of events, chance, or simply good luck. For me, when I consider the timing and the sequence of events that were necessary to make my early retirement happen, I am sticking to my belief in the Lord's intervention. Logic would say I was a fool to retire in the first place. The entire chain of events started only ten months earlier when Dorothy and I first discussed the possibility of retirement against seemingly overwhelming odds. As John Slosar said on receiving approval of my transfer to FACC, "You must have someone looking after you."

Saying goodbye was different this time; I was not moving to another location, nor would I likely cross paths with these friends another day. This leaving was for good.

I took the opportunity of my farewell speech to look back on my thirty years as a Ford employee and shared so many pleasant memories of the company and the people. It truly is a Ford Family. I was privileged to work with and for exceptional people doing interesting and challenging work all over the world.

What more could you ask for in a career? In some ways, I felt like I was losing my best friend, but I was excited to learn what God had planned for Dorothy and me in the future. There was no standing ovation—just the appreciation from my peers for a job well done.

Leaving my parking space for the last time on February 25, 1988, was when my emotions got the best of me. I stopped the car in the parking lot for a few minutes. With a lump in my throat, I thanked God for all the great years he had given me with Ford. I pondered with amazement how God once again had directed my choices. What would the outcome have been if I had contested moving to my new position last January upon returning to DPO from the task force?

There are numerous references in the New Testament comparing the life of a Christian to participating in a race, persevering until the finish line is reached. In Acts 20:24, Paul says, "…my only aim is to finish the race and complete the task the Lord Jesus has given me…." This race is not a sprint but a marathon; all of us tire and stumble along the way, but thankfully, with the help of others and by the grace of God, we are refreshed and encouraged to press on toward the goal. I do not regard my retirement from Ford as the end of the race; rather, it was a pause for me to catch my breath before racing onward toward the greater goal.

Being an automotive person, I make the following analogy, Ford provided the vehicle, no pun intended, for Dorothy and me to spread the Gospel. We got aboard in 1957 and had numerous stops along the way to fulfill God's purpose. On March 1, 1988, we reached our final destination with Ford and were now waiting for the next bus. What a wonderful journey it has been. No matter your status or position in life, we all have a special gift to spread the Gospel.

Identify your vehicle and get aboard. The price has already been paid by Jesus Christ's death on the Cross.

# CHAPTER 11: FROM CORPORATE LIFE TO FISHING

*"Let us not become weary in doing good, for at
the proper time we will reap a harvest if we do
not give up." Galatians 6:9*

*True Blue 31-foot Tiara in
Onekama, Michigan, 1984.*

It had only been two weeks since my retirement from Ford—not long enough for me to fully realize that I was retired and embarking on a career as owner and operator of my new business, True Blue Charters. Dorothy and I were busy packing again, not the entire household with furniture and all, as with our former relocations around the world, but only what we would need to be comfortable for a six-month stay. It was time-consuming work nonetheless as seasonal clothes and personal items that would assure our comfort had to be sorted to take from our home in Northville, Michigan, to our condo across the state in Onekama. We had bought the condo in 1984 while I was still at Ford and had kept our base in Northville, but now Onekama, two hundred miles and a four-hour drive to the north, would be our residence during the charter fishing season from April through October. After four years of recreational fishing out of Onekama, I was about to launch a charter fishing company.

## PRINCIPLE 4: PASSION.

Passion is when you love what you do and why you do it. Passions are an integral part of forwarding your purpose—the fuel that drives the gifts God has given you. God will combine your gifts and passions to help you accomplish your purpose. Many people think they must search for their passion, but the truth is, it is already inside of you. First Corinthians 10:31, "So whether you eat or drink or whatever you do, do it all for the glory of God."

Passions may change, but the purpose remains the same. In my case, witnessing to others about Christ was my purpose; my passion for my work at Ford and my passion for fishing were different, but the purpose was the same. I believe Dr. Martin Luther King said it best, "If a man is called to be a street sweeper, he should sweep streets even as Michelangelo painted, or Beethoven composed music, or Shakespeare wrote poetry. He should sweep streets so well that all the hosts of heaven and earth will pause to say, here lived a great street sweeper who did his job well."

You might say that God had been preparing me for this charter fishing company all my life. My passion for fishing began during my early years and was nourished by fishing in waters around the world—Venezuela, Brazil, Australia, and New Zealand.

By nature, I think fishermen have an affinity for God's creation, a love for the outdoors and the creatures that inhabit it. Fishing at dawn with the sun rising, I was so often taken with the beauty of the world, a truly a religious experience for me. Romans 1:20, "For since the creation of the world God's invisible qualities—his eternal power and divine nature—have been clearly seen, being understood from what has been made, so that people are without excuse." Over the years, I found many opportunities to use fishing to witness about Christ to those around me, either by word or deed. I have always been inspired that Christ's first four disciples—Peter, Andrew, James, and John—were fishermen. Christ gave their passion a new purpose, "Come, follow me," Jesus said, "and I will send you out to fish for people." Mark 1:17.

During the six years between returning to the US and my retirement, I had taken many friends and family fishing for walleye, perch, and salmon. Taking people out was not new, and I thought the big difference now was that I would be paid for my efforts. I was soon to learn there were many differences between taking friends fishing and having a customer pay for your expertise and expecting you to produce results. When fishing with friends and not catching fish, I could always fall back on "you should have been here yesterday." This quip no longer worked. A paying customer wants to know, "What are you going to do today so that I land a good catch?" Fishing for fun and fishing as a business are akin to cooking hotdogs on a grill and serving as an executive chef at the Waldorf Astoria.

*True Blue*, my thirty-one-foot Tiara which I had purchased in 1982 without any thought of establishing a fishing company, was already equipped with electronics, downriggers, and fishing tackle for salmon fishing. Beyond this equipment, I still had a lot missing for a viable company, foremost among them was learning to establish and run a charter business. Apart from the fishing, there is marketing, obtaining commercial insurance and licenses, and preparing for and passing safety inspections from the United States Coast Guard and State of Michigan—just to name a few of the tasks I now had to master. I was soon to realize the transition from a corporate background with its vast resources at my disposal to being a sole proprietor was a daunting task. For the first time in years, I was out of my comfort zone. I was twenty-four years old when I joined Ford, and I had the thirty years to hone my skills and build my reputation. Now, I was fifty-five as I embarked on a new career which I thought I understood but quickly realized I did not.

In short order, it struck me that I had a steep learning curve if my business was going to survive and be profitable. Charter fishing is hard work, physically and mentally. You could say it called for age-appropriate responses. As with professional athletes whose careers are determined by the physical demands of their profession, I understood that my success would be limited by my physical responsiveness. At the "young" age of fifty-five, many charter captains are thinking retirement, not starting a new business. I was physically fit for my age and had no doubt about being able to perform the duties of a charter captain for the foreseeable future; nevertheless, I decided to establish a short transition period of two to three years to prove that I could physically and fiscally establish a sound business. If I could not do it, then what?

I was about to find out.

My biggest challenge was redefining my business goals and my ministry. I took inventory of the skills I had acquired over thirty years at Ford: making quick and complex decisions, planning business processes and growth, reading a balance sheet, evaluating return on investment, and wielding people skills. I determined many of the skills I had acquired at Ford were valuable, but I was still not sure how to apply them to a one-man operation. There were no corporate policies, audit requirements, or higher-level approvals to guide my decisions; my opinion was the only one to direct action. Learning from my mistakes instead of applying company policy was how I would learn to operate, and I hoped to learn fast enough not to "sink the boat."

There were some less tangible but crucial skills—perhaps you could call it attitude—that I had picked up: having a passion for what I did, giving one hundred and ten percent to every effort, and conducting myself with honesty and integrity. I knew these attributes would be essential in running my own business and fulfilling God's purpose of telling others about the love of Jesus.

Using skills I had acquired at Ford, I developed a balance sheet and business plan for True Blue Charters. I calculated I needed around twenty charters per season to break even. With a relatively short season of four to five months, knowing that I needed a minimum of twenty to break even, I set my goal to run thirty charters to ensure an operating profit: income from charters less fixed and variable costs. In addition to profit, thirty charters would assure a steady cash flow. The established charter businesses were running sixty to eighty charters per season. I hoped I could eventually achieve those numbers, but for the first season, thirty seemed a realistic goal. Having my Ford pension to fall back on provided a financial cushion, but I had decided if I could not cover my expenses and pay myself a nominal wage after two to three years, I was in the wrong business and God did not want me there. If a large income was my goal, I could have stayed at Ford where I would make more in a few months than I could chartering all year!

My goals certainly included being solvent with True Blue Charters as it was important to achieving a larger purpose: I wanted to use my fishing business as a ministry to witness to those around me just as I had done during my thirty years at Ford. My passion for fishing was the same: using my boat, *True Blue*, to be God's ambassador and witness to those around me about Christ. Since that first summer of 1984 when we docked the boat at Onekama Marine, it had been my home port, where I had docked and stored my boat and from which I now proposed to operate my business. Walking the one hundred yards from our chalet at Pirates Cove to where my boat was docked was too good to give up. In addition, I liked the marina and had friends there.

I had chosen to put *True Blue* in the water as soon as the ice was gone on Portage Lake in April 1988 to prepare the boat and fishing gear for my first salmon season as a charter captain. Before the season opened, I booked several charters for later in the season. I also fished several times a week with friends and my new first mate, a high school senior in Onekama, to ensure I was ready for my first paid charter on May 28, 1988, with Hunter Pickens, my former boss in Ford Asia Pacific. His trip was "for real." Despite fishing several years with friends, this would be my first paid charter. I did not want anything to go wrong. My first mate and I were excited as we had prepared well and were ready for the beginning of my new career.

Overall, my first summer as a charter captain went well, including my first charter with Hunter Pickens when we caught ten chinook salmon. I ran a total of twenty-eight charters, most of them with people I knew. A small number of customers came by referrals from friends or other charter captains. I also added a few trips, gratis, for family or as fund raisers for local organizations such as the Lion's Club and our Portage Lake Charter Boat Association. I had not yet been able to do the kind of marketing and advertising to see results beyond these bookings. I hoped more charters would come the following season from mailing brochures, word of mouth, and winter boat shows. Looking back, I realize my first charter season was more like fishing with family and friends. With this experience, chartering was going to be a piece of cake, or so I thought—funny how things have a way of coming back to bite you. I had yet to experience the difficulties from customers whose rowdy behavior and excessive drinking proved a challenge in future seasons.

The most important lesson I learned during that first season was paying attention to details. When I was a pilot, I performed essential pre-flight checks to ensure a safe flight, and now I had a checklist to follow before starting *True Blue's* engines. On one occasion when my customers arrived at the dock at five a.m. ready to depart, I realized I didn't have enough fuel to run the charter. Fortunately, Jim, the owner of the marina, showed up at six a.m. and personally fueled my boat (not a good way to impress the marina owner after he reluctantly agreed to let me base my charter business at his marina). Another time, I forgot to empty the toilet holding tank. It was not until a customer used the toilet the next day that I remembered, and a bucket served the purpose (not the way to impress female customers). The list of mishaps is longer, but each taught me a valuable lesson. While I never had a written checklist for the boat as I did for the plane, I learned to follow an exact routine after each charter (check fuel, holding tank, fishing tackle, clean boat) and the following morning (check for ice, running lights, electronics, proper lures). I also continually reminded my first mate to ensure everything was in order. On the plus side, we had a few great catches with customers. Sometimes, I even surprised myself and my fellow charter captains, but of course, I never let on.

After my first season ended in October and the boat was placed in storage, I assessed my progress toward my goals. If my first year was any indication, I was ahead of schedule. I had run enough charters to make a small profit, my customers were pleased with the fishing experience, and some had already booked for the coming year. Apart from small glitches, there were no major problems that caused me to re-evaluate my business plan. Listening to some of the problems other captains had to deal with, I concluded I was either lucky or particularly good at what I was doing. After a successful and enjoyable 1988 charter season, I concluded, "What could go wrong?" I was about to learn the truth of Proverbs 16:18, "Pride goes before destruction, a haughty spirit before a fall."

Another carryover from my Ford days was keeping good records. From the day of my first charter, I began taking notes. I recorded customer information: name, address, phone number, email address, names of children, and anything else that would make our relationship more personal. I also took photos on each charter and a group picture of the family and their catch. In December, I sent out my first newsletter to each customer with photos included, being sure to mention names of customers and notable incidents such as first or biggest fish. Several customers wrote back to thank me for the newsletter while others mentioned it when booking their next charter. I did not recognize it at the time, but this first step to personalize my business would become the foundation of my success.

# CHAPTER 12: BECOMING A CHARTER CAPTAIN

*"I will instruct you and teach you in the way you should go; I will counsel you with my loving eye on you." Psalm 32:8*

*(left to right) Dennis and Billy Pate in Mazatlan, 1990.*

One evening in December 1988, Dorothy and I had just finished dinner at our home in Northville when I received a call from a Ford colleague, Lee Sanborn. He related how negotiations to sell Philco-Ford Brazil were underway and Ed Launberg, managing director of Philco-Ford Brazil, for whom I worked during my assignment to Brazil from 1979 to 1982, had specifically requested me to come to Brazil to help with the compensation and benefit negotiations. I was at a loss for words; the thought of returning to Brazil had never entered my mind. The offer of a six to nine-month contract at my previous salary with all expenses paid was generous. I would travel to Brazil as necessary and maintain an office at the Ford World Headquarters using DPO staff for administrative assistance as needed. My first thought was, "Thanks for thinking of me, but no thanks." Having worked with Lee on DPO staff before I retired, I felt comfortable saying, "Lee, it is the furthest thing from my mind, but let me talk it over with Dorothy and I'll call you in the morning." Dorothy was as surprised as I was when I told her. Apart from winter exhibitions at fishing shows to attract new charter clients, it was a slow time of year. The money would be good, and it was not a long-term commitment. I had to admit talking about Philco-Ford Brazil and my time working in Brazil rekindled my enthusiasm for the corporate life I once lived so successfully, and the negotiations would place me once again in the midst of a fray. If I accepted, it would be like old times. I also was flattered that my expertise as a troubleshooter and negotiator was still in demand at Ford.

As we talked about all of this, Dorothy said, "Why don't you go? I know you would enjoy it."

The next day, I signed a six-month contract at Lee's office and was on my way back to Brazil by the end of the week. The trip rekindled a spark in me that I thought had been extinguished. I wondered, "Had I retired too soon? Was this the life I still wanted?" I was about to find out!

In the coming months, I made three trips of about ten days each to Sao Paulo. During the last trip, in June 1989, we reached an agreement with Itautec, a Brazilian banking and investment firm, and upon government approval, the agreement was signed the following October.

Negotiating the sale of Philco-Ford Brazil was bittersweet. I had worked for that company, so seeing old friends and reliving the past brought back fond memories of our time there. I drove by our former house in Morumbi, the soccer stadium where Dennis and I saw many games, and Calvary International Church where our friend, Bill Fawcett, had been pastor. Mario, the son of our former maid, Maria, was still working at Philco-Ford Brazil where I had gotten him a job, but Maria had retired, and I was not able to contact her due to my limited time in Brazil.

Participating in the negotiations reminded me of the sale of Ford Tractor in 1986 and Ford Aerospace and 1987. I had represented Ford interests and, at the same time, advocated for Ford employees to receive the best compensation and benefits possible from the new owners. The 1988–89 Brazil negotiation posed a particular concern as Philco-Ford Brazil was the company that I helped to grow by launching a new plant in Manaus. I knew and worked with many of the Philco-Ford Brazil employees. For the most part, employee interests were protected during the sale, and I felt comfortable with the compensation and benefits we had negotiated with Itautec.

When I returned home after my first trip to Sao Paulo, I thanked Dorothy for encouraging me to go. I was glad I had taken the assignment. By the time of my third and last trip to Sao Paulo in June, however, I told Dorothy I knew this was my last assignment with Ford. I did not want to give up the freedom of running my own fishing business and being outdoors for a return to the corporate life. I had needed that one last negotiation to know for sure it was time to cut my ties with the past. Any doubt I had about retirement was gone. God had never been wrong before, and he was not this time. My transformation from the corporate man to the charter captain had received a big boost, and I was now focused on the future and what God had in store for us in the fishing business.

The fishing shows from the previous winter paid off. I had forty charters booked for the summer of 1989, many booked at the shows. Compared to my previous season when I knew most of my customers personally, over half of my 1989 charters were first-time customers I did not know. How quickly things can change. The first two charters of the season were with new customers, and both proved a disaster. Based on the previous season, I had been lulled into a false sense that all customers were easy to please; I was in for a rude awakening.

The first group, four buddies in their mid-twenties from Ohio, showed up late and hung over from drinking too much alcohol the previous night. They carried a large cooler filled with beer on board. I hesitated about letting them bring the cooler of beer on the boat but decided not to make it an issue. After all, they were paying customers. We had hardly left the dock when they began opening beers and became loud and rowdy. Soon after setting the fishing lines, they wanted to know when the fish were going to start biting, to which I laughed and told them to be patient.

"That's why we call it fishing, not catching," I said. From the looks on their faces, they did not think it was funny. After another ten minutes and another beer, one of the customers became belligerent and rude to both the first mate and me. I asked him to behave. Two of his friends asked him to be quiet. He complied for a few minutes but then started complaining again. I stepped out from behind steering wheel and politely but very firmly said, "If you just want to drink beer, it's a lot cheaper to go to a bar than on a charter. You fellows decide, but if you stay, I expect you to behave in a civil manner."

"You've got to be kidding!" the unruly customer replied.

With that, I asked the first mate to pull the lines. "We're going in!"

That set the customer into another tirade.

135

"If you don't stop, I am calling the sheriff to meet us at the dock." Under maritime law, a ship's captain has the ultimate authority for the safe passage of his vessel and the persons on board. I personally never had to follow up on such a threat, but I know several captains who did.

Immediately, he quieted down. No one said another word during the forty-minute ride back to the dock. As unhappy as I was with their behavior, I pro-rated the charter fee and told the group if they ever wanted to come back without the beer, they were welcome. My decision to pro-rate the fee was perhaps foolish, but I never doubted it was the right decision at the time—something about turning the other check or doing unto others.

I allowed my desire to run a charter to cloud my better judgement to provide a safe and comfortable environment for my customers. In my rush to establish myself as a charter captain, I had not fulfilled my responsibility and had overlooked the basic purpose I was doing this—to witness to customers about the love of Jesus Christ. It was not the first time I let my enthusiasm get the best of me and would not be the last. A time for patience was in order. In my humiliation, I prayed for forgiveness in putting my pride first and not seeking God's wisdom.

From my Christian perspective, I welcomed anyone on the boat; I believe they were there for a reason. However, as I had just experienced, there are times when turning down a charter is best for everyone. I needed to ensure that prospective customers understood what I considered acceptable conduct when they booked the charter, not when they were boarding *True Blue.*

My son, Dennis, and several of his friends helped as first mates on *True Blue* that summer. The wages and tips were good, but getting up at four-thirty a.m., seven days a week, turned them off. It was difficult to find first mates who were willing to stick with the job. Since Onekama was a small port, most first mates were local high school or college students looking for summer work. I was fortunate to find excellent young men and women to work for me.

I soon learned that each captain has his own "secrets" as to how fast he runs his boat with different lures, how deep and how far behind the boat he trolls lures, and the list goes on. In other words, each captain and boat crew develop their own technique of what works best for them. There are so many variables in fishing you never learn them all. Just when you think you have fishing all figured out, you get surprised with something new. I learned to keep detailed daily records of my fish catch to identify some of the variables and adopt what worked best for me under given conditions.

By the end of the 1989 season, I had run forty-five charters and was beginning to see myself as a successful charter captain. I had suffered some setbacks and difficult learning experiences, but I also had some successes. I was more attentive in my bookings and more confident in my ability as a captain. I had achieved my two-year goal of establishing a profitable charter business, and most importantly, I knew without a doubt this was my new ministry.

The highlight of the 1989 fishing season was not about fishing. On August 25, 1989, our daughter Luanne was married to Pat Letarte. I will never forget reading 1 Corinthians 13 at her wedding with tears in my eyes. My little girl was now a beautiful bride! The years had passed so quickly.

Beginning in the early 1990s, a new segment of the market was emerging: people who wanted a quality family recreation experience. Being new and without a backlog of experience holding me back, I was one of the first charter captains in our area to focus on that customer base. Being a family man, I was already thinking and feeling the change as evidenced by the number of family charters I was booking. These customers still wanted to catch fish, of course, but other criteria were becoming equally important such as enjoying the environment, time with family, and the quality of the charter. Consequently, the cleanliness of the boat, the courtesy of the captain and crew, the safety equipment, the privacy of enclosed toilet facilities, and a willingness to teach the parents and children how to catch a fish all added to the quality of the charter. It was no longer strictly a fishing business; it was a recreation business competing with other forms of recreation for consumer dollars. I could feel, and my data confirmed, that my charter business was taking roots; my reputation for quality service and a family-oriented business was paying dividends. I ran almost sixty charters the summer of 1990 with over half being families and repeat business.

One of the toughest decisions I had to make as a charter captain was when to cancel a charter due to weather. Over time I developed a feel for when I should cancel or reschedule as I had many repeat customers and knew their tolerance for *mal de mar*. Also, the presence of children made a difference; I did not want to ruin their fishing experience with rough seas. When customers had motel reservations and a bad weather forecast for the dates of their charter to complicate matters, I notified them that I would call with a final scheduling decision the day before they left home. Even then, sometimes I cancelled and wished I had not, and other times I did not cancel and wished I had.

I identified two additional new markets to expand my charter business: fly fishing and women. Fly fishing has historically been viewed as a freshwater sport, but catches of saltwater fish on a fly were gaining attention in the fishing community. Also, the perception that women were not interested in fishing was changing. With increased media coverage, more women were coming into the sport each year. The problem was these markets were in states that bordered on salt water, not on Lake Michigan. Was this a nudge by the Holy Spirit that Dorothy and I were heading south? With Luanne now married and Dennis working full time and going to school, Dorothy and I found ourselves with freedom from parenting and time to move about.

Since the market was growing in the saltwater sphere, the idea of winter fishing was drawing me to Florida. With that thought in mind, in November 1990, Dorothy and I went to Mazatlán, Mexico, for a week-long fly-fishing school put on by Billy Pate and Jack Samson. After considering the overall cost of the trip and the school, Dorothy and I agreed it was an investment in learning saltwater fly fishing. An added incentive may have been the beautiful area we were to visit. Mazatlán, a city of over 250,000 in the 1990s, was a rapidly growing tourist destination located on the Pacific coast. Mazatlán reminded me of the coastal cities of Venezuela, white sandy beaches, tropical climate, and great fishing.

Billy Pate was one of the foremost big-game fly fishermen in the world. He was one of the pioneers of fly fishing for tarpon and sailfish in the 1980s and held the world record with a 188-pound tarpon on the fly. Jack Samson was equally well known as a writer, WWII war correspondent, editor, and fisherman. During his tenure as managing editor of *Field and Stream*, it became the foremost sportsman's magazine in the world.

On the first day, Billy and Jack taught us knots, casting, and rod handling techniques. The last two days were spent on the water fishing for sailfish and putting into practice what we had learned. I could not help but think how I might apply these techniques to a new business in Florida. For now, I would just learn and enjoy my time.

The "Bait and Switch" technique developed by Billy Pate uses hookless baits—usually mullet, ballyhoo, or other smaller bait fish—behind the boat. When the sailfish bites one of the hookless baits, the first mate slowly pulls the bait away teasing the fish to follow. With the fish at the back of the boat, the mate quickly reels the bait into the boat as the captain puts the boat in neutral, and then the angler casts his fly to the fish. If all goes well, the sailfish will take the fly and the battle begins. Many times, the fish is within ten to fifteen feet of the back of the boat when it bites the fly. I thought light-heartedly, "I wish I could figure out how to coax salmon to the boat!" Unfortunately, I never figured that one out.

The second day, Billy and I were the only two on his boat; the two other anglers had to catch a flight home. It was a slow morning with only one fish seen. Billy and I chatted about his career in fishing and how blessed he had been over the years to lead such an interesting life. After lunch, Billy and I were relaxing since it was a beautiful day, calm and sunny with the low rumble of the diesel engine lulling us to sleep. Suddenly, the mate shouted in Spanish, "*Pez vella* [sailfish]!" I jumped to my feet and picked up the fly rod. Even with sunglasses reflecting the sun, it was difficult to see the dorsal fin of the sailfish piercing the sparkling water at sixty feet behind the boat. The sailfish came in striking at the bait with its bill as the mate slowly retrieved (teased) the sailfish to the boat. My heart pounded. The mate lifted the bait from the water as the captain put the boat into neutral. I cast several feet in front of the sailfish: one, two, three strips, retrieving the fly, when suddenly the sailfish turned on the fly, its bill protruding a foot out of the water. The line came tight, and I set the hook with an aggressive strip strike, pulling hard on the fly line in my left hand. Immediately, the sailfish leaped clear of the water twenty feet behind the boat. "*Que hermosa vista* [what a beautiful sight]," the first mate shouted with the sun reflecting off the water droplets and the iridescent colors of the sailfish. After twenty minutes, several more jumps, and coaching from Billy, we had the sailfish to the boat. The mate took the fish by the bill, removed the hook, and carefully lifted the fish on board for a picture. Compared to the marlin and yellow fin tuna I caught in Australia, sailfish are not as big and powerful, so they can be handled safely if handled with care.

Billy and I would have put the fish back in the water, but the local practice was to keep the catch for food. As it was my first sailfish on a fly, we agreed to keep the fish, take pictures, and give it to a market for local consumption.

One of my prize possessions is a picture of Billy Pate and me with my first sailfish caught on a fly. Since that day, I have caught over forty sailfish on a fly, and not restrained by local custom, I have released all of them. None of those catches were as memorable as that first one with Billy Pate.

I asked Doug West, my buddy from Onekama, if he would like to accompany me to Costa Rica in February 1991 to check out the area and do some fishing. Doug had never fly fished before but was eager to accompany me.

As most charters did not provide fly fishing tackle, Doug and I flew to Miami a few days before our trip and bought twelve weight fly rods and reels from Worldwide Sportsman, a tackle shop in Islamorada, Florida, owned by Billy Pate himself.

Doug and I flew from Miami to San Jose, Costa Rica, on February 17, 1991. Doug was fun to be with as nothing ever seemed to bother him, a kind and generous person.

Costa Rica, a country of approximately 4 million people, has the most stable political and economic system and the highest literacy rate in Central America. San Jose, the capital city of approximately 280,000 with the lowest crime rate in Central America, is regarded as safe.

We checked into the Wet Dolphin Hotel, *Dorado Mojado* in Spanish. The hotel was new, its two-story cement blocks painted a bright yellow and a hand-painted sign of a large dolphin over the front entrance. After settling into our nicely appointed rooms, we contacted our charter captain and spent the afternoon sightseeing. In the center of town was a large two-hundred-foot wooden wharf in need of repair. In the 1950s the wharf was used to load bananas onto cargo ships destined for the US, but eventually, the banana company moved elsewhere, and the port closed. Moored next to the wharf were several boats including our charter boat.

Over the next three days, we caught and released six sailfish ranging from seventy to one hundred pounds each. On our last day,

Doug hooked a blue marlin he had fought for over an hour. I poured buckets of seawater on him to keep him cool in eighty-degree tropical heat. We had the fish close to the boat when the reel locked up and Doug lost the fish. I made two additional trips with friends to Costa Rica in 1992 and 1993 but none as memorable as that first trip with Doug.

We had another big event on September 3, 1991, the birth of our first granddaughter, Emilee Ann Letarte. Little did we realize how much joy a grandchild would bring to our lives.

During those first five years—1988 to 1993, I felt like I did thirty-five years earlier when I started at Ford. Learning new skills, earning the respect of my peers, and meeting new people was exciting and satisfying. On top of it all, I loved what I was doing. The same traits that I learned at Ford applied to my charter business: hard work, integrity, and respect for people. My transformation from a corporate executive to charter captain was well on its way. There were some mistakes along the way—I like to call them learning experiences—but overall, the progress in growing my fishing business was evident. The one constant throughout the past five years was that God was in control: closing the door on returning to Ford as a consultant, redirecting my salmon charters to a family-oriented business, and widening the door to Florida. No matter the change in circumstances, when you need direction, ask God. Isaiah 30:21, "Whether you turn to the right or to the left, your ears will hear a voice behind you, saying, 'This is the way; walk in it.'"

# CHAPTER 13: SOUTH TO FLORIDA

*"For we are God's handiwork, created in Christ*
*Jesus to do good works, which God prepared in*
*advance for us to do." Ephesians 2:10*

*Dorothy and Dennis*
*at the new house in Florida, 1993.*

The winter of 1993, Dorothy and I made a one-week trip to
Florida to "look around" and determine if a saltwater fishing
business was feasible during the winter months. We fell in love with
Charlotte Harbor on the west coast of Florida. On our last day before
returning to Michigan, we purchased a home in Riverwood, a new
golf course development on Charlotte Harbor. When we got back to
Northville, we listed our house with a broker, trusting it would sell
by the time our house in Florida was built. Dorothy commented,
"Can you believe it? In one week, we explored the west coast of

Florida, found a location where you could start a fishing business and I could golf, and bought a house?"

I said, "Normally, I would say 'no,' but knowing how God has opened doors for us around the world to serve his purpose, yes I do."

I had arranged to pick Mom up from the Wyandotte Hospital after a four-day stay for an irregular heartbeat. At two a.m. the day of her release, I received a call from the hospital telling me Mom had fallen getting out of bed and broke her hip. She was in surgery, and I should come as soon as possible. After the surgery, I stayed with Mom in her room, and by six a.m. she was alert and asking when she could go home. I felt so bad for her; she had anticipated going home and being in her own apartment again. I explained she had broken her hip and needed therapy to gain more strength before going home.

A few days after surgery, Mom reluctantly started physical therapy at the hospital, but despite daily encouragement from Dorothy and me, she just did not have the strength nor the will to continue. She kept asking to go home, so Dorothy and I picked up Mom from the hospital. We did not want to put Mom in a nursing home. I called my brother Tom, and he suggested I bring her to his home in Frederick, Maryland. Tom's wife Joann had worked as a nurse in Frederick and had numerous medical contacts in the area. Tom and Joann had a large four-bedroom ranch house with room for Mom and easy access to the outside. Our home in Northville had no downstairs bedrooms, and Mom was unable to climb stairs. Mom would have preferred to stay in her apartment but realized that was not possible. On March 21, Mom and I flew from Detroit to Washington, DC, sixty miles from Frederick. At the time, there were no direct commercial flights into Frederick Municipal Airport. During the flight, Mom and I talked about the farm, Dad, Grandma, and Lawrence, our hired hand on the farm who had become part of our family; they were all gone now—how times have changed. I sensed Mom knew we did not have much longer together. Tom met us at the airport where we talked over lunch for an hour. I had a return flight to Detroit later that afternoon, and Mom was tired from the trip. I hugged Mom for a long time before saying goodbye; I did not know if I would ever see her again.

Dorothy and I kept in touch with Mom, calling every week to talk to her. Tom said Mom was losing strength but otherwise holding her own. We flew to Florida in June, and everything was on schedule for completion of our house by September. I called Tom from Florida to update him on the purchase of our new house, and he told me Mom was not doing well. He and Joann were concerned how much longer they could care for her at home. Tom encouraged us to continue with the house as it had no bearing on Mom's care whether Dorothy and I were in Michigan or Florida.

Dorothy and I were still in Florida when our realtor in Michigan called that they had a buyer for our home in Northville. What great timing, we thought. The realtor faxed the closing documents to us at the motel in Port Charlotte where we were staying. Before signing the documents, Dorothy and I talked. Who would have thought we would be moving again? Well, we still had our condo in Onekama which we would return to in the summers for salmon charters. We knew God was in control and had another ministry for us in Florida. We were concerned for Mom. We wanted her to come with us but knew that was no longer possible. The Lord has never let us down; we had no reason to believe this would be any different. We signed the contract and returned the documents to our realtor. There was no turning back now.

Back in Northville, I contacted Palmer Moving and made plans for shipping our household belongings to Florida. Some of the employees we knew from our previous travels with Ford twenty years ago were still working for Palmer and said they would take good care of us.

Tom called in August to say they were moving Mom to a nearby nursing home as they no longer could meet her medical needs. I called Mom several times and tried to encourage her. I told Mom we had kept the apartment in Riverview for her when she was ready to come home. She replied, "No, Son, it's time for me to be home with the Lord." Tom, Joann, and their kids visited Mom almost every day. I told Mom that Dorothy and I would come to visit after Labor Day as soon as the charters slowed down.

Tom called on September 13, saying Mom had taken a turn for the worst and we should come to say goodbye. The following morning, Dorothy and I made the twelve-hour drive to Frederick, not saying much, praying for Mom, and reliving our memories. We drove straight to the nursing home to see Mom. She was not able to talk but acknowledged us with a weak smile. I held Mom's hand as I prayed with her for about an hour. The nurse suggested we let Mom rest and come back in the morning, so Dorothy and I kissed her goodbye and headed to Tom's house. Tom and Joann had not come with us as they wanted to allow us time alone with Mom. We had just arrived at Tom's house when the phone rang. Joann and Tom were out shopping for groceries, so I answered. The nurse said Mom passed away just after we left the nursing home. I hung up and hugged Dorothy; we both cried. Tom and Joann were disappointed they had not been there; we both knew Mom was just waiting to say goodbye before she went to be with the Lord.

The next morning, I arranged to bring Mom to Michigan where she would be buried next to my dad who went to be with the Lord in 1963. It did not seem possible it was thirty years ago; I felt older.

As Dorothy and I were driving home from the funeral, I felt so blessed to have a mom like her. Much of who I am today is because of her and my dad. As with my dad, I wished I would have spent more time with Mom as she grew older. She was so proud of

Tom and me, as we were of her. I will tell both Mom and Dad when I see them in heaven.

We returned to Florida at the end of September, and the house was right on schedule. I wish Mom could have come to stay with us; she would have enjoyed it—just like her trips to Venezuela and Australia. Over the past weeks, I had been researching flats boats and decided on a twenty-foot Action Craft, a quality flats boat made in Cape Coral, Florida, not far from Port Charlotte. Paul Gard, owner of Action Craft, advised me that Gulfwind, a sixty-boat marina in Cape Haze near Boca Grande, was a dealer and was looking for a guide to promote Action Craft. Headquartered in Sarasota, Gulfwind had several large Sea Ray dealers in Florida.

The next morning, I stopped by Gulfwind and met the sales manager, John Snyder. John was a natural-born salesman, tall and lean with a big smile and easy disposition. He said Paul Gard had called him to give me a guide discount on the boat.

It was common practice for guides to trailer their boat and launch at public ramps to keep costs down. Not wanting to launch and retrieve the boat every day at crowded public ramps, I asked John if he knew a place to keep the boat on a hoist; he knew of none. John said I could keep the boat in the water at the marina, but I did not like that idea due to the rapid growth of algae on the bottom. He then said, "Let's go talk to Terry." Terry Lynch, owner of Gulfwind, was a fireball—short and stocky, balding, and in his fifties. He purchased Gulfwind six months previously and was determined to grow the business. We chatted for a while, and I could tell by Terry's can-do attitude this was a place I could do business.

I related my concern about leaving the boat in the water, and Terry agreed. "No problem," he spouted, "we can put a boat hoist in the marina." Terry then led me outside to show me the perfect location for my boat hoist right next to a popular seafood restaurant and the water taxi to luxurious Palm Island Resort. Customers and guests had to walk by my boat to the restaurant and the water taxi.

Terry said, "I'll pay to put in the hoist and lease it back to you for a fair price." I thought for a minute and said, "Two hundred dollars a month." Without hesitation, Terry said, "It's a deal," and we shook hands. I was a little taken aback; it was almost too good to be true. I wanted to sign a lease contract, but Terry said, "No problem. We have a handshake; that's good enough for me." I was thinking for my own protection but did not have the nerve to discuss it further. That handshake was the only contract we had until I left Florida fourteen years later. Terry and I went back to his office, and I ordered my new Action Craft with a two hundred horsepower Mercury outboard. With Terry's help, I was put on the Mercury Pro Staff with a discount on the motor. As I drove home, I thought God must really want us here!

We joined the golf club at Riverwood, and Dorothy played golf every day. She was the Ladies Club Champion nine of the fourteen years we were in Riverwood. We also bought a golf cart for Dorothy to play golf and get around Riverwood. Dorothy and I visited several churches and found an Assembly of God Church that became our church home until we left Florida.

I went to Gulfwind the day after we arrived in October, and sure enough, there was my Action Craft setting on a boat hoist just as promised by Terry Lynch. My first impression was right; this was going to be a good place to do business! Back country fishing would become my favorite. The thrill of sighting a fish and casting to it with a fly or artificial lure is hard to beat.

The first few months I fished everyday by myself to learn the area. It is easy to get lost if you are not paying attention. Charlotte Harbor and Pine Island Sound cover miles of shallow grass flats interspersed with mangrove islands. Tides are a critical part of fishing the back country. Some days at low tide there is not enough water to float the boat, while at high tide the water would be two to three feet deep in the same area.

Stealth is essential when fishing in one to five feet of water, so I poled the boat using a twenty-two-foot graphite push pole while standing on a poling platform mounted above the outboard engine. When fishing water too deep to pole, I used a twenty-four-volt trolling motor mounted on the front of the boat.

In October, Terry Lynch introduced me to Dean Beckstead, owner of the exclusive Palm Island Resort located directly across the Intercostal Waterway from Gulfwind. Palm Island is just that, an island privately owned by Dean Beckstead and the condo owners. Palm Island provided water taxi service to and from the island departing from Gulfwind, or people could use their own boats. Dean introduced me to many residents on Palm Island who became good customers. Over time, we became good friends, and I oversaw Palm Island's fishing program, arranging charters and providing fly casting lessons for Palm Island residents and guests.

Wanting to increase my proficiency in fly casting, I signed up for the Federation of Fly Fishers Casting Instructor Certification Program where I met Captain Sandy Melvin, owner of Gasparilla Outfitters on Boca Grande. The instructor, Steve Rajeff, was a legend in fly casting and had won the World Fly Fishing Championship several times. Sandy and I learned casting mechanics, motor skills, and teaching techniques on how to cast. The second day we practiced casting and critiquing each other on our casting stroke. I was intimidated yet impressed with the knowledge and skill required to be a good fly fisherman. Sandy and I were among those who passed the course. We were proud to get certified as fly-casting instructors by none other than Steve Rajeff, the master himself. In 1995, Sandy became a certified Orvis Dealer, and I provided guided fishing trips and fly-casting instruction for his customers.

Pat, Luanne, and Emilee plus Dennis came to Florida over the holidays. It was nice to be together as a family in our new home. I could not help but think of Mom and how I missed her not being

149

there. I do not recall a Christmas or Easter that one—if not all—of the family, including Ron and Ina and their kids, did not come to Florida while we were there. I enjoyed taking them fishing and seeing the porpoises and manatees.

Setting up my new charter business in Florida was like starting over again. There was a lot to learn: a different boat, fishing techniques, species of fish, rules and regulations, and new customers. I reflected on the similarity of the skills required to run a fishing business and my early days at Ford—the passion for my work, learning new skills, meeting new friends, and, yes, making a few mistakes along the way. All the same skills applied to a different venue.

Starting in January 1994, I was booked several times a week. Some were customers from Michigan, but the majority were new customers from Florida. My networking was paying off. By the time Dorothy and I returned to Onekama the first week of June, I had run sixty-eight charters in Florida. The highlight of that first spring was my first tarpon on a fly. I had the day off and decided to take my eleven-weight fly rod and check out a new area called Johnson Sholes just south of Boca Grande Pass. It was early May, and the tarpon were starting to show up in large numbers on the Gulf beaches. I was idling along the sholes enjoying the beautiful morning when I saw a school of tarpon, maybe a dozen, moving toward me in four to six feet of water. I put the throttle in neutral, shut off the motor, and waited. The tarpon were swimming slowly toward me, stopping occasionally to circle and stir up sand near the bottom. I used the trolling motor to position myself for a cast as they approached within sixty feet of the boat. Standing on the bow, I cast the tarpon fly; it was too far to the right of the tarpon. On the second cast, I hesitated as the fly slowly sunk to the bottom. I stripped (retrieved) twice with my left hand and saw a tarpon move toward the fly. The line came tight. I pointed the rod at the fish while striking hard with my left hand to drive the hook home. The tarpon exploded from the water thirty feet from the boat twisting and turning, the silver-dollar-size scales reflecting the sun. My natural reaction, learned while sail fishing, was to point the rod at the fish allowing slack in the line so as not to break off the fish. Then another jump and another, each one more acrobatic than the previous. The fish took off, peeling sixty yards of line off the reel.

Everything was happening so fast, there was no room for error with a hundred-pound tarpon on a fly line. I finally stopped the fish and began to gain line. Being alone, I was at the mercy of the fish. After fighting the fish for about twenty minutes, I used the outboard motor to move closer to the tarpon and regain line. Another fifteen minutes and I had the estimated eighty-pound tarpon alongside the boat with the leader in hand when the leader broke just a few inches above the hook where the tarpon's raspy mouth had weakened it. I sat back, exhausted but happy and content. I was going to release the fish anyway but wanted to remove the hook. Sorry, no pictures, you must take my word for it. What a great way to end my first full season of fishing in Florida.

We arrived back in Onekama the first week of June just in time for the steelhead fishing on the "scum line" fifteen miles offshore. During the early summer months of June and July, as the lake water warms from the sun, thermal bars form on the surface in the deeper cold water of Lake Michigan. The deepest part of Lake Michigan, almost 1,000 feet deep, is approximately thirty miles offshore due west of Onekama. In early June, the thermal bars are encountered closer to shore as the water warms from the shoreline westward. You know when you cross one as the surface temperature drops from five to fifteen degrees Fahrenheit within a few hundred feet; a surface temperature in the forties would not be uncommon. The water visibly churns where the warmer, lighter water encounters the colder, heavier water and comes to the surface. The colder water holds debris and insects that the fish feed on, hence the name "scum line." Trolling for the acrobatic steelhead with in-line planer boards

151

on the surface is exciting and productive. The only downside is the colder water sometimes produces fog, even on a bright sunny day.

It was my first charter of the season in Onekama and what a memorable charter it would be. We ran into the fog about ten miles offshore where the visibility was reduced to approximately three hundred feet. *True Blue* was equipped with state-of-the-art radar, so we had not been concerned fishing in the fog. We were catching numerous steelhead and having a good time when I noticed a target on the radar three miles off my port bow. It was not uncommon to see other boats on the radar moving at trolling speed; however, this vessel was closing at a high rate of speed. Even with radar, a good rule of thumb is to proceed at a speed commensurate with the visibility and be able to stop within half the distance of the visibility. The boat on my radar was obviously travelling at a cruising speed in the twenty-mile-per-hour range. As the vessel closed to within two miles, I maintained course to establish the relative bearing. If the relative bearing—the clockwise angle in degrees from the heading of your vessel and a straight line to the other vessel—stays the same and the distance is decreasing, you are on a collision course with the other vessel. It appeared the other vessel, now one-half mile distant, would pass behind us. I asked my first mate and the customers to keep a close lookout. Visibility was about three hundred feet when suddenly the cruising boat came out of the fog headed right at our port bow. I instinctively turned to starboard trying to avoid the collision. Just as I thought the boat was going to hit us, it veered hard to our port. We could see the bottom of the boat in a tight starboard turn away from us and hear the deafening roar of the motors as it passed within fifty feet of *True Blue* and taking my three in-line planer boards and lines with them. Then it was quiet, except for the sound of my idling engine. We were in semi-panic mode, and I asked if everyone was all right. Thank goodness they were. I asked my first mate to quickly take in the other lines. I did not want to stop and risk tangling them in the propellers. There appeared to be no damage other than the loss of the planer boards. As soon as our lines were in, I trolled in search of the other boat, my first mate shouting, "Is anyone out there?" To which we heard a faint reply, "We are dead in the water." I shouted, "Are you ok?" and again heard the reply, "Go to channel 68." I switched to channel 68 just as they were calling me to ask if we were alright. I replied we were and was about to let my angry emotions loose on them when the caller said it was Tony on the boat *Fishin Time*. I could not believe it; Tony was a respected charter captain and friend from Portage Lake Marine across from Onekama Marine. I said, "It's me, Denny, on *True Blue*." Tony said, "Oh my God, I'm sorry." Tony explained he was on another boat from the Portage Lake Marina showing the owner how to fish for steelhead. When they started home, visibility was over a half mile. Tony noticed the fog settling in again and asked the owner to slow down, but they were still going too fast for conditions. Tony had just taken the wheel and was slowing down when they saw us dead ahead. Had he not been at the controls, Lord knows if the inexperienced owner would have been able to avoid hitting us. My fishing line and planer boards had caught in one of the propellers. Tony was going under the boat to see if he could cut the line off the propeller rather than go fifteen miles home on one engine. I told Tony we would stand by until we knew the outcome and offered to help if need be. As upset as I was, I could not leave a stranded boat out there. About fifteen minutes later, Tony called on the radio to say the line was cleared from the propeller and they were back on two engines ready to head home. I asked my customers if they had enough energy to fish some more, and without hesitation they said, absolutely! We fished another hour, catching several more steelhead before starting home. Fortunately, after a few miles, the fog lifted, and we had a relaxing trip back. Not letting an opportunity to witness pass by, I commented how fortunate we were to not have been hurt or killed and how Tony had taken the wheel at just the right time. I related some of my past experiences and how the Lord had looked after me and my family over the years—not all good times—but we knew He was always there with us. To that I got a collective, AMEN!

Luanne called to let us know she was expecting another child in October—our second grandchild. We returned to Florida in late September, and Dorothy flew to California in October to be with Luanne when our grandson, John, was born October 28, 1994. We were so happy for them and thanked the Lord for another healthy grandchild. The bad news was we had to put our yellow Lab Buffy down. I knew it was coming, but knowing does not make it any easier. For the first time in fifteen years, we did not have a Labrador in our family.

I have always been fond of animals, particularly dogs. Buffy was the third Lab we had put to sleep, and each time I would recall when we had to put our Great Dane to sleep on the farm when I was sixteen years old. I cried then, and I still do now. I promised myself Buffy would be the last; I did not want to go through that pain again. However, soon after we returned to Florida and the grief had subsided, I found a breeder that had yellow Lab pups available. Dorothy and I went to look at them and left with a yellow female which we named Daisy.

# CHAPTER 14: EXPANDING MY BUSINESS

*"In the same way, let your light shine before others, that they may see your good deeds and glorify your Father in heaven." Matthew 5:16*

*(left to right) Jody Moore and Dennis, crevalle jack, 1998.*

Fishing was a growing industry in Florida with more guides coming into the business every year. With increased fishing pressure came the need for more fishing and charter regulations. In December, approximately twenty guides from Clearwater to the Everglades attended a meeting in Tampa and formed the Florida Guides Association to represent our interests. After discussion, we elected a board of six guides, of which I was one. Scott Moore, a prominent guide from Sarasota was president, and Van Hubbard from Charlotte Harbor was vice president. At the end of our first year, membership increased to over seventy guides. From its humble beginning, the organization has grown to over one hundred and fifty members throughout Florida.

By January 1995, I was busy every day with charters and fly-casting seminars at fishing shows and local fishing clubs. Phil Benton, past president of Ford and my former boss at Diversified Products Operations in Dearborn, had just retired to Florida and called me for a charter in February. It was a cool windy day, but we had a great time chatting about old times and friends at Ford. Phil still had a boat of his own in Michigan, and we both laughed when I reminded him how the DPO general managers asked me not to bring up boating in their meetings with Phil as he preferred talking about boating rather than their business priorities. Phil chartered with me several more times over the ensuing years.

On one occasion when I had just returned from a charter and was putting my boat on the hoist, a gentleman walked up and introduced himself as Larry Hardy, bull pen coach for the Texas Rangers baseball team. Larry was staying in a condo next to Gulfwind and wanted to book a charter. This was the beginning of a new friendship and a new source of customers. In his fifties, Larry was athletic with black hair and a southern accent. Before his coaching career, he was a star pitcher for the University of Texas and several major league teams. The Charlotte County Baseball Stadium in Port Charlotte had been the spring training site for the Texas Rangers since 1988. Over the next five years, I could count on twenty charters each spring from Larry and the other ballplayers. Will Clark would be the best known as an all-star first baseman with the San Francisco Giants and Texas Rangers. Roger Pavlik and Bobby Witts, both starting pitchers, were also regulars, fishing several times each spring. In 2003, the Rangers moved to a new spring training center in Arizona, and I lost touch with most of the players.

I had my first serious encounter with a hammerhead shark the spring of 1995. Sharks are abundant around Boca Grande Pass, and it is not uncommon to lose a hooked tarpon to a shark. My customer had hooked a large tarpon and had it alongside the boat after a thirty-minute fight. I was leaning over the side to remove the hook when the water exploded. I was drenched and could hardly see with saltwater dripping down my sunglasses. The tarpon bolted away from the boat, pulling the one-hundred-pound fishing leader from my hand, and almost pulled the unsuspecting angler over the side. I instinctively reached up and cut the line with my pliers just as a large hammerhead passed within two feet of the boat in pursuit of the tarpon. I looked up at the angler and said, "Nice catch," as we both sat for a minute to catch our breath. A side note: the world record 1,060-pound hammerhead shark was caught from a flats boat in Boca Grande Pass on May 23, 2007.

Pat and Luanne and the grandkids moved back to Michigan that spring. The real estate market in California was depressed, forcing Pat to look for other work. I suggested they move into the condo in Onekama until they decided what they were going to do, and they gladly accepted. It was great having them around during the summer, especially the grandkids, Emilee and John.

Fly fishing can be a snobbish hobby if you let it. Having the most expensive fly rods, reels, and gear is part of the ambience. That is not to diminish the almost religious experience that many anglers have for fly fishing, including me. It has been said that fly fishing is to fishing as ballet is to dancing. The movie *A River Runs Through It* cannot say it any better.

My fishing world expanded when Don Beck, a retired businessman from Wisconsin, called to say a local tackle shop had recommended he call me for a charter. This would be the beginning of a long personal and fishing relationship. It was October 1995 when Don asked me if I still had contacts in South America to fish peacock bass. I mentioned Brazil and Venezuela as probably the best in the world since I had fished them both extensively when I lived there. Don then asked if I would be interested in organizing a trip and coming along as the travel guide and bag carrier. He was thinking of asking two friends, Don Volk and Bob Voell, to go with him. After further discussion, I agreed I would consider it and get back to him.

Dorothy thought it was a great idea and did not mind me leaving for a week. She was playing golf every day and socializing at the golf club. I checked with outfitters in Manaus, Brazil, and found one that would be perfect. The *Amazon Queen* was a large three-deck river boat set up to accommodate twelve anglers. We would eat and sleep on the boat and fish from eighteen-foot skiffs with outboards that were towed behind the mother ship. Each skiff would have its own guide with two anglers. We would fly from Miami to Manaus, board the *Amazon Queen* in the afternoon, and cruise north on the Rio Negro during the night. The next morning, we would be at our first fishing destination ready to fish. I talked to Don, and we agreed to schedule the trip in January 1996.

The next few weeks, I put together tackle and lures for us to take. Spinning or baiting casting rods and reels capable of handling fifty-pound braided line was essential due to the dead trees and underbrush in the water we would be fishing. The lure of choice was a top water plug known as a buzz bait with a small propeller on the front and back to create commotion in the water. The technique was to cast among the fallen stumps and bushes that lined the shore and retrieve as fast as you could with big sweeps of the rod to create turbulence in the water. I took my eight and nine weight fly rods in hopes of getting a record peacock bass on a twelve-pound tippet.

We left Miami at midnight on January 5, 1996, and arrived in Manaus at five a.m. Eastern Standard Time the following morning, a distance of 2,400 miles. The captain greeted us at the airport and took us to the mother ship for breakfast and introductions to the other eight anglers on the boat. The *Amazon Queen*, eighty-five feet in length, was built in 1989 as a floating hotel and had all the comforts of home. We departed Manaus about noon for the fifteen-hour trip north on the Rio Negro. The next morning after a good breakfast, we boarded our skiffs and headed out to fish. Don Volk and I had not fished fifteen minutes before Don had a heart-stopping bite, a large peacock bass cleared the water a few feet from the boat. Peacocks are hard fighters, and the bite is furious. I had several bites on my eight-weight fly rod with an orange fly but could not stop them on my lighter fly tackle before they reached cover.

The *Amazon Queen* practices catch and release to protect the species; however, we kept enough for a meal the first night, and it was delicious. Back at the mother ship that evening everyone related stories of the fish that were caught. I could only tell of the ones that got away. I had brought four dozen large flies but lost a dozen that first day. The fish liked orange and yellow colors, so the cook let me use some food coloring to dye my flies. The second day, everyone but me caught lots of fish; I lost five or six nice fish in the bushes again. The third day, Don Beck and I fished together, and I suggested to him that we remove the hooks from his lure and when he got a strike, I would immediately cast my fly to the spot where the bites occurred. We could fish farther away from the bushes to give me a better chance at landing a fish. After several casts, the water boiled behind Don's hook-less lure. I immediately cast to the boil, and on my second strip the line stopped with a thud. A large peacock came flying out of the water, and the fight was on. I played the fish in open water, and after a ten-minute battle brought the fish to the boat. The fish weighed fourteen pounds, just ounces short of the world record on twelve-pound tippet. Don and I were happy, and after high fives, we took pictures and released the fish. I caught a few smaller fish that day using the same technique, each one a memory. Back at the mother ship that evening, I put the fly rod away, satisfied with what I had come to do. The remainder of the trip, I caught numerous peacock bass on spinning tackle but none as rewarding as my fourteen-pound fish on the fly.

During our five days, we proceeded up the River Negro about sixty miles in beautiful and isolated country. We passed four or five huts along the river during the entire trip—local families living off the jungle. After the fifth day of fishing, it was time to head back to Manus. It would take us all night and the better part of the next day to arrive in Manaus and catch our flight back to Miami. It was a great trip with good food and excellent fishing and accommodations. Don and friends wanted to do it again next year. I agreed. For me, it was like old home week coming back to Manaus and fishing for peacock bass. It brought back memories of when we built the Philco plant in Manaus in 1981. I would have liked to spend more time in Manaus, but our schedule did not permit it. I was pleased with how quickly my Portuguese came back; by the time we left I was conversing with the locals like I had never left.

I returned from Brazil just in time for a large fund-raising banquet at our Assembly of God church in Port Charlotte. The church was involved in a large building program which they completed in 1997. I remember the first Sunday in our new building some four hundred members filed in singing Amazing Grace. The amazing thing was the church was not a penny in debt. Dorothy and I had come to know many in the church, and the music program was the most talented of any church we attended. The week-long Christmas pageant—with live donkeys, camels, and sheep—attracted several thousand from the Port Charlotte area. We attended a Bible study at Riverwood with others we had met at church. No matter the country, the city, or the state Dorothy and I have lived in, we have been blessed by the Christian love and fellowship of brothers and sisters in Christ.

Life at Riverwood was good. Dorothy played golf every day, and we had great friends and neighbors. Several Riverwood residents fished with me when their families came to visit. I did not play golf but was grateful Dorothy did as it provided me the opportunity to fish and not feel I was neglecting her. I know she felt the same as when I had a few days off Dorothy would ask, "Isn't it time for you to go fishing again?"

We did not return to Onekama until mid-June in 1996; the emphasis had shifted to Florida. Most of my Onekama business was now repeat customers with a few new referrals from friends.

The fall of 1996, I took Don Beck and his friends on a second trip aboard the *Amazon Queen*. It was as successful as the trip earlier that year with lots of fish and great food. I made one major change. The captain would drop us off at Barcelos, a small town of about 18,000 on the Rio Negro noted for the exotic tropical fish exported around the world. A charter flight would then fly us back to Manaus in an hour and a half instead of the seventeen hours by boat we experienced on the first trip. We would have time in Manaus to sightsee and have dinner before our flight left at midnight for Miami. Manaus had grown since I was there in 1981. We took a taxi to the Philco plant, but we did not go in for lack of time. From the outside, the plant looked the same as I remembered it. As I gazed silently at the plant, my thoughts drifted back to 1981 when we launched the new plant and my return to Brazil in 1988 to negotiate the sale of Philco-Ford. Were my friends still working there? How was business? What products were they making? But I digress—I was thinking on the way home how blessed I was that I could return to fish the Rio Negro and see Manaus again.

After returning to Florida, we discussed going to Venezuela the following year instead of Brazil. Don would let me know soon so we could make plans.

During the 1997 season, I fished with Blaine McCallister, a professional golfer on the PGA tour, and Mike Mularkey, former professional football player and NFL coach. I had over one hundred trips on the books through mid-June.

Dorothy and I were back in Florida by end September 1997. The pattern of four months in Michigan and eight months in Florida (30–40 fishing trips in Michigan and 100–120 fishing trips in Florida) was a perfect balance for us. My purpose for starting a charter business was to provide a ministry witnessing to customers. I liked fishing by myself, and I really enjoy the company, but it is not a ministry. With customers on the boat, my passion was about the people, getting to know them as friends and sharing my faith in Jesus with them. My boat became my mission field. I was careful not to sound "preachy" but let my actions and words reflect my walk with Jesus. Matthew: 5:16, "In the same way, let your light shine before others, that they may see your good deeds and glorify your Father in heaven." I think Christians too often view a mission field as being far away, but it is also the neighbor next door, the people you encounter each day, or the customers on your charter boat.

I made three fishing trips to Venezuela with Don Beck and his friends—in 1998, 1999, and 2000. The most memorable was our last trip in January 2000. I finalized plans for Don Beck, Don Volk, Bob Voell, and me to fish the Guri Reservoir, one of the largest impoundments in the world—1,641 square miles—covering forests that are now excellent habitat for peacock bass.

We flew from Miami to Caracas and on to Ciudad Bolivar, the capital of the State of Bolivar. The next morning, we made the seven-hour trip from Ciudad Bolivar, where the Guri Dam is located, to the fishing camp. Never again, we thought. The road was two lanes and bumpy, a long, hot ride in a dilapidated van with no air conditioner. The accommodations at the fishing lodge were basic. Large spiders roamed about, and fortunately, we had screens on the windows as the mosquitos were bad at night. The boats were old aluminum eighteen-foot skiffs with a sixty-horsepower outboard. The guides could not speak English but knew how to fish. We all had stayed in worse accommodations, so if the fishing was good, we would be happy.

The fishing was excellent with lots of ten-pound fish. We were releasing up to twenty per person each day. I caught several on the fly, but as in Brazil, the fish preferred the noisy top water baits. It did not take long for my Spanish to come back while chatting with the guides, and I was in constant demand to explain things to my "gringo" friends. Meals turned out to be excellent as were the lunches they packed for us each day. After dinner, we prepared for the next day and went to bed early. I reminded everyone to keep an eye out for the spiders just as we turned out the lights. They were big enough you could hear them walking. One night, Bob Voell was roaming around with a flashlight and thought he heard one!

Things took a turn for the worse on the third day. The boats had radios necessary for safety. Don Beck and I were fishing together when I heard a call come over the radio in garbled Spanish. I could not make out exactly what was said, but it had to do with an accident. Our guide turned to us and said one of the other anglers had been hooked by a lure, and they needed help. I translated the message to Don Beck; he groaned and said, "I bet it's Bob Voell. I knew I shouldn't have let Bob fish with Don." Don Volk had a reputation for being careless with his casting. When I fished with Don in Brazil, I gave him plenty of room. We motored fifteen minutes to the other boat, and there was Bob with a lure attached to the top of his head pinning his hat in place. It looked funny, but it was not. Apparently, Bob stood up just as Don was casting and *wham*, both sets of treble hooks sunk into the top of his head. I had some experience removing hooks but, after surveying the damage, felt Bob should see a doctor. We had to cut Bob's hat off around the lure so the wind would not pull on it while running under power. He was obviously in pain, and I was a concerned he might go into shock.

The owner had been contacted by radio and was waiting for us when we arrived at camp. The closest medical facility was a two-hour drive. A driver and van were waiting to take Bob to the medical facility, and Don Volk insisted he go with Bob. Having spent time

163

in the interior of Venezuela before, I was concerned as to the quality of medical care Bob would receive.

Don and Bob left at five p.m.; it was now ten p.m. Dinner was over, yet we had no word from them. There was not much we could do but wait and pray for him. About twenty minutes later, the van arrived. Bob's head was in a bandage. They had to cut out the hooks and stitch up the wounds. They gave him antibiotics and said he would be fine. Everyone was just relieved to see them. The owner graciously provided Bob with a hot meal after he returned. Bob slept in the next morning while the rest of us went fishing. Overall, we had a great time despite the accident.

We left on a positive note; the owner of the camp arranged for a charter flight to take us to Ciudad Bolivar, a forty-five-minute flight compared to the seven-hour drive. The plane, an Antonov An-2 made in Poland, is popular for its durability and short-field landing and takeoff performance in the underdeveloped countries of the world. With a wingspan of sixty feet and body length of forty-two feet, it has a 1,010-horsepower radial engine and a dual wing. It was worth the trip just to ride in a plane like that.

Upon arrival at the airport in Caracas, we were told our flight back to Miami had been rescheduled to the following morning due to mechanical problems. The airlines did not offer to pay for overnight accommodations, so we found a hotel near the airport at our expense. Having the afternoon free, we hired a taxi to do some sightseeing. Maiquetia was noted for its beautiful beaches, resorts, and big game fishing when Dorothy and I lived there in the 1960s. We would take Luanne and Dennis to the Macuto Sheraton Resort for a weekend with friends. Dorothy and the kids would spend time on the beach while I went fishing for striped marlin on a local charter boat. It was a mecca for expensive sport fishing yachts from the US and Caribbean during the peak of the marlin season.

What I saw was only a remnant of how I remembered it. Several of the resorts, including the Macuto Sheraton, and marinas were closed, and the area was rundown. You could see the economic and political situation was taking its toll on the country. We were told by the taxi driver that travel was becoming difficult and unsafe in the country; tourism had diminished.

Waiting at the airport the next day, I recalled the good times and friends we had while living there. We had fond memories of the people and the country; it was difficult to see the negative changes that were taking place. I could not help thinking of Dorothy's folks, John and Lucille Hacker, who tragically lost their lives in Maracaibo in 1969. We departed Caracas on December 12, 2000; I knew it would be my last time in Venezuela. It would be good to be home for Christmas.

# CHAPTER 15: FISHING WITH FAMILY AND FRIENDS

*"And God is able to bless you abundantly, so
that in all things at all times, having all that you
need, you will abound in every good work."*
*2 Corinthians 9:8*

*(left to right) Ed Marinaro and Dennis
Grand Champion Redbone Tournament, 2002.*

On March 7, 1998, my good friend Chuck May and I flew from Miami to Cancun, Mexico. I had been offered a special rate for two at the Casa Blanca Fly Fishing Lodge on Ascension Bay on the Yucatan Peninsula. Special rates were often given to travel agents and outfitters in the US to promote their business. I was apparently on the list as I received numerous offers from fishing lodges throughout the Caribbean, Central, and South America. It was a forty-five-minute charter flight from Cancun to the lodge located right on Ascension Bay. Everything about the place was first class:

accommodations, food, boats, and guides. We fished for three days and caught a variety of fish each day. I thought the lodge had possibilities for a future trip with Don Beck or other customers and would get the word out when I returned home.

Since my first overseas trip with customers in January 1996, I continually refined my role as travel agent, translator, and fishing guide; however, organizing the trip, airline tickets, visas, and local accommodations was time consuming. In addition, I was responsible for the safety of my customers. I enjoyed the trips, as did my customers, but I needed a different business model to alleviate the stress and time commitment. For future trips, I resolved to advise when necessary but all arrangements would be the responsibility of the angler. I would be paid a modest guide fee to help each angler prepare for the trip and catch fish after arrival. It was a win/win for everyone. Anglers had the benefit of a fishing guide they knew and trusted for a minimal cost, and I had the pleasure of fishing around the world and witnessing about Jesus.

It was a warm and sunny morning in mid-April 1998 as we motored along the beach looking for tarpon. Jody Moore, a well-known fly fisherman and contributing editor for the *Florida Sportsman* magazine, and his friend were looking to catch a tarpon on the fly. At the same time, Jody and I both spotted a vortex in the calm water and the large dark shape of a school of fish. "Too small for tarpon," I said. Jody agreed and thought they might be permit. As we moved closer with the trolling motor, Jody said, "Holy cow! It's a school of crevalle jack, maybe twenty-five to thirty pounds." Jody quickly put down his twelve-weight fly rod and picked up his eight-weight fly rod, perfect for that size fish. The fish were moving in a circle much like tarpon on the surface. Jody made a perfect cast right in front of the school and stripped slowly—nothing. He picked up his fly line and cast again; on the third strip the line came tight. There were no jumps, typical for a crevalle jack, just a screaming run that peeled one hundred yards of line off Jody's reel. Pound for pound, crevalle fight harder than any fish I know. Fortunately, they are not good to eat and not targeted for food fish. I have often targeted them with fly fishermen due to their hard fight but never caught one over twelve to fifteen pounds. After forty minutes of give and take, Jody, wet with sweat, had the fish close to the boat. Each time I reached for the tireless fish, it moved away. Finally, I got a firm grip on the tail with my gloved hand and eased the fish over the side of the boat. We took a few pictures, weighed the twenty-six-pound crevalle jack, and released it back into the water. We wondered if this could be a record on twelve-pound tippet (leader). Jody found out later it was close but not a world or state record, even if it was in our minds. My reward was a center fold feature photo and article written by Jody in the *Florida Sportsman*. You cannot buy that kind of advertising!

After returning to Riverwood in October 1998, I sold my Action Craft and bought a new Pathfinder flats boat with a sixty-horsepower Mercury. It was smaller and lighter than the Action Craft. There was only one small bait well for shrimp and two watertight compartments. It would be ideal for myself and two anglers. The Pathfinder ran in four inches of water and was easier to pole, but the flat bottom would make for a rough and wet ride in open water. I would have to forgo some tarpon trips on the beach due to weather. I decided to give it a try. The boat would be ready to pick up the next week. I had already made it known I was selling my Action Craft and had a buyer lined up. Don Beck was my first customer in the Pathfinder. After adjusting to the cramped space, Don liked the boat. In fact, he went out and bought one. I ordered it for him direct from the factory. Don was now fly fishing regularly, and we took second place in the Gasparilla Outfitters Fly Fishing Tournament in November.

Winter tides are the lowest of the year in Charlotte Harbor. On mornings with a strong offshore wind, the back country was hard to reach at low tide. With a four-inch draft, I could run or pole almost anywhere I wanted to go. The low tides force the fish into potholes, and if you can reach them, it is, "like shooting fish in a barrel." As the tide rises and the fish begin to move back out over the flats, tailing redfish feeding on small crabs are easy targets. For about two hours after low tide, it is a fly fisherman's dream. Sometimes I would get out of the boat and wade in six to eight inches of water pushing the boat and angler into casting range. I knew of only two or three other guides that could get back where we fished.

On February 25, 1999, Luanne gave birth to her third child, Grace. Dorothy went to Lebanon, Ohio, for two weeks to help Luanne with the baby. Three grandkids, who would have thought it! Dorothy and I agreed grandchildren are special and give you a new definition of love.

That winter with the Pathfinder was great fun, and my fly fishermen loved it. One morning, Don and I were skimming across the flats when we ran out of water and came to a sudden stop. Fortunately, I had the steering wheel to hold onto, but Don went flying to the front of the boat. I instinctively reached out and grabbed him by the leg as he went by or he would have gone headfirst into the water. Thankfully, the Pathfinder has a small recess in the transom called a tunnel which protects the propeller from damage in shallow water.

As spring came, I began to see the downside of my Pathfinder. It was a two-man boat: me and one customer. Some of my regular customers who wanted to take a family member or friend had a hard time on the boat. There were also days when I could not fish the Gulf for tarpon as the flat bottom was not comfortable in a chop. I borrowed a friend's flats boat a few times to allow me to take an extra angler or get along the beach for tarpon.

I began to doubt the wisdom of my choice and started looking for other options. Hell's Bay Boatworks was started in 1997 and used a new technology to build the hull—Kevlar and carbon fiber instead of fiberglass—which made the hull light, ridged, and almost indestructible. They were expensive compared to fiberglass due to the material cost and production process. I called the factory and discussed my requirements for a boat. They thought their boat would be just what I was looking for, and they would like to put me on their guide program. As I would be heading back to Michigan soon, we agreed I would take a trip to see the factory when I returned in October 1999.

The highlight of the summer was the Onekama Marine Fishing Tournament. Luanne, Pat, and Dennis fished with me every year, and Emilee, John, and Grace joined in from the time they could walk. Fishing was a family event we all looked forward to each summer. On a few occasions, family ties were strained when the kids came back to the condo complaining to Dorothy that they were not going to fish with Dad again because he hollers at them. In the end, they kept coming back. We did well, winning a few times, but the memories are what really count.

Another tradition for our grandkids started in 1998 when our granddaughter Emilee went to the Covenant Bible Camp located next to Onekama Marine. The camp, an extension of the Covenant Church, is based on a Christ-centered, one-week camping and recreation program for children aged seven through high school. As John and Grace became of age, they also attended the camp each summer. All three never missed a year of camp through high school.

In August 1999, I took Dennis to Alaska for his graduation present. He graduated from Eastern Michigan University with a Bachelor of Science in Facilities Management that spring, and I wanted us to go while we had a chance. He had taken a position with Blue Cross/Blue Shield of Michigan in 1998 and was getting busier at work. First, we flew to Anchorage and spent the night. The next morning, we flew to Port Alsworth, an hour southwest of Anchorage.

Fishing Unlimited is a fly-fishing lodge located on Lake Iliamna, home to some of the best trout fishing in Alaska.

Everything about the trip was first class: rooms, food, guides, and fishing. We flew to a different lake or river each day. The pilot was our guide; we would land on the water, taxi to shore, and begin fishing. It was all catch and release on flies. We caught Dolly Varden, grayling, rainbow trout, and silver salmon depending on the location. One day, we flew to Kodiak Island and fished a remote inland lake for Dolly Varden and grayling. The weather was typical for Alaska: sun, clouds, rain, and cold depending on the day.

The highlight of our trip, however, was not the fishing. At times, we fished rivers frequented by brown bears looking for fish. On those occasions, anglers would move out of the water to let the bears go by; no one argued over territory with them. The guides gave instructions on what to do if you encountered a bear: wave your arms and shout; do not turn and run.

The third day, we saw several bears at a distance, nothing to be concerned about. Dennis and the guide were fishing one side of the river, and I had crossed to the other side to try a different spot. The river was quite swift and deep, so I had to pick a shallow spot to cross. I was standing in the river up to my thighs about forty feet from shore catching rainbow trout when I looked up and saw a bear walking along the riverbank. He moved into the tall grass and disappeared, so I went back to fishing. Suddenly, I heard Dennis and the guide shouting. I looked up, and there on the bank was a large brown bear. I had a camera hanging from my neck, and without thinking I put my fly rod under my arm and started taking pictures as the bear came down into the water directly toward me. The bear had its nose to the water looking back and forth; it did not acknowledge I was there. As the bear moved closer, I heard Dennis shout, "Wave your arms and shout at the bear." The guide ran to the shallows where I had crossed; he was armed with a forty-four-magnum revolver strapped to his side.

I was mesmerized and continued to take pictures as the bear advanced to where I could have touched it with my fly rod. I could not back up as the river was too deep and swift. I shouted as loud as I could, and the bear stopped, looked at me, then turned, and slowly walked back to shore before disappearing in the tall grass. After a minute, to regain my composure, I slowly walked to shore, watching for the bear as the guide was making his way toward me along the riverbank. He was half mad and half glad. He admonished me for not shouting at the bear right away but acknowledged taking a stand facing the bear and not panicking was the best thing I could have done. Even Dennis thought this trip may not have been such a good idea.

Back at the lodge I was the center of discussion, not for catching fish but for being so careless as to almost get eaten by a bear. The pictures turned out great by the way. Dennis and I caught lots of fish that week; Dennis swears he caught more than I did—a little father/son competition. Overall, it was the most enjoyable and memorable trip I have ever been on. Thanks, Son, I will never forget it.

In the fall of 1996 Dean Beckstead of Palm Island Resort asked me if I would take the owner of *The Angling Report* for a few hours of fishing as part of an article he was doing on the resort. I met the owner, Don Causey, at the Palm Island docks. He was not just the editor but was an avid fly fisherman that had fished the world. *The Angling Report* focuses on assisting and educating the travelling angler on when and where to fish based on the actual experiences of subscribers. It is highly regarded in the fly-fishing community. Don and I talked about our overseas fishing experiences while releasing a few snook and headed in for dinner at the resort. Don suggested we keep in touch and perhaps we could do business together in the future. I thanked him and told him I enjoyed fishing with him. Based on the recommendation I got from him in his January 1996 monthly newsletter, he must have enjoyed our trip also. From time to time, I would hear from him about trips he thought would be worth checking out. He recommended the Casa Blanca trip to Ascension Bay that Chuck May and I took in March 1999.

In November, Chuck and I made our first of five trips to Deadman's Cay on Long Island in the Bahamas. We took a flight from Miami to Nassau, and then a connecting flight to Deadman's Cay. The flight ran twice a week and was not always on time. Accommodations were basic but clean with three separate apartments in a one-story building. Meals were delivered to the door by a local restaurant; the food was good but not always delivered on time. We both agreed it was worth a trip back.

My last trip to Deadman's Cay in 2004 was unforgettable but for the wrong reason. The second day, I got a blister on my heel from a shell in my wading boot. I had numerous cuts and nicks wading in bare feet in the back country in Florida, but they all eventually healed; this one did not. By the time we were ready to come home four days later, it was infected and was very painful.

We arrived in Miami about midnight, and I could hardly walk. The redness and swelling had spread up into the calf of my right leg. After a four-hour drive to Port Charlotte, I went to the Emergency Room at five a.m. The doctor did minor surgery on my heel to see if there was anything in the wound and put me on the strongest oral antibiotic he could give me. He said it was a viral infection and could be serious if it continued to spread. He sent me home with strict orders to soak my foot in a solution he gave me and to report back the next day. If there was no improvement, he would admit me to the hospital and start an intravenous antibiotic treatment. Fortunately, the next morning the swelling and pain began subsiding, so we stayed with the oral treatment. It took a month before the wound was healed.

In February 2000, Don Beck, Tom Balisteri, his son Jim, and I went to Golfito Bay in the southern-most part of Costa Rica, bordering on Panama. The area adjacent to the Golfito National Wildlife Refuge had just opened to tourism and fishing. We stayed at Crocodile Bay Resort, a newly constructed facility capable of handling twelve guests in luxurious accommodations. A friend of mine knew Todd Staley, who used to guide in Charlotte Harbor and was now the director of fishing at Crocodile Bay. I contacted Todd by phone, and he arranged for us to come to Crocodile Bay at an attractive discount. In return, I was to teach local captains the bait and switch technique.

We arrived on February 10. The area was breathtaking—the aqua blue of the Bay of Golfito edged with the plush greenery of the rainforest opening into the blue waters of the Pacific. It was a nature lover's paradise. The lodge had one twenty-eight-foot boat with a single diesel inboard capable of getting offshore. Several other smaller boats were used to fish in Golfito Bay for snook, rooster fish, and reef fishing. Don, Tom, and Jim decided to fish Golfito Bay while I went offshore with a local captain and two mates to show them the bait and switch technique used by Billy Pate.

We set up our teaser rods and started a westerly troll looking for signs of bait and birds to alert us of fish in the area. I demonstrated how to rig a hookless bait, tease a sailfish, and present the fly by the angler.

During the morning, we saw a few sailfish, but none came to the teasers. About noon, a sail came up behind the left teaser. The mate quickly took the rod and teased the sailfish, slowly at first, until the fish saw the bait and then coaxed it to the boat. The captain put the boat in neutral just as the mate lifted the teaser out of the water, and I made a cast. Before I could start picking up line, the sail turned and took my fly. My first strike was when the fish was airborne ten feet behind the boat. A couple more strip strikes, and the fish was on. After an aerial display, the fish ran and then sounded. The inexperienced captain was not able to keep the boat in position at first. Giving him instructions in Spanish while playing the fish was difficult, but in a short time the captain was doing fine.

After about forty minutes, I had the fish close to the boat, just below the surface, and swimming slowly with the boat. We decided to take the fish by the bill, lift it aboard for pictures, and let it go. One mate took the leader in hand and was gently leading the sailfish to the boat while the other mate leaned over the side to take the bill when the leader broke. For a moment, the fish did not know it was free and kept swimming along with us. We all stared hopelessly at the fish as it slowly moved off and down out of sight.

Word spread that we had lost our sailfish, and by the time we got back to the dock, a crowd was gathered to welcome us. It would have been the first sailfish on a fly at Golfito Bay Lodge. The rest of the trip was anticlimactic for me. Tom landed a nice rooster fish, and his son Jim took a sixty-pound yellow fin tuna offshore. All the guests enjoyed fresh sushi and grilled tuna over the next couple of days.

In May 2000, Chuck May and I made a trip to Guatemala. My friend, Don Causey of *The Angling Report* had called to say the fishing was the best he had seen. We travelled from Miami to Guatemala City and stayed overnight. The next morning, we were met by a representative of the Fins n Feathers Inn and transported by van to Iztapa on the Pacific Coast, a trip of about two hours through tropical scenery. On the van with us were four anglers from Brazil; I had a great time trying to practice my Portuguese.

The inn was surrounded by a high wall with armed guards at the gate; crime was a problem in the country. Once inside, it was nice with an open veranda and dining room overlooking the marina. The accommodations and food were excellent. We left the marina at seven a.m. the next morning and proceeded about a mile on a waterway to the Pacific.

We fished the same bait and switch technique used in Costa Rica. The captains and mates were setting phenomenal records for sailfish releases; thirty a day was not uncommon. Chuck and I released thirty-one sailfish over three days, not counting those we lost. We were tired puppies when we got back at night. Overall—accommodations, quality of the boat, captain and crew, the weather, and my friend, Chuck—it was one of the best trips I have ever been on. The only one I enjoyed more was my trip to Alaska with my son Dennis.

In July 2000, Dorothy won the Michigan Senior's Golf Championship, the pinnacle of her golf career. Dorothy's golf had improved significantly since our return to the US in 1982. Playing regularly at the Washtenaw Golf Club and Riverwood, where she was club champion multiple times, Dorothy had improved to a three handicap. She was playing in numerous tournaments around the country and was tough to beat in competition. I am glad I did not take up golf; I do not think I could handle being second all the time.

Upon returning from my trip to Venezuela with Don Beck and his friends, in December 2000, I picked up my seventeen-foot Hell's Bay flats boat and sold the Pathfinder to a friend at the marina. As with my Pathfinder, I decided not to give my Hell's Bay a name as I was changing boats every other year. Anyway, I already had my thirty-one-foot Tiara, *True Blue*, back in Michigan.

The Hell's Bay would do all that I needed. It floated in four inches of water, poled like a leaf on the water, was quiet, had an adequate live well, would handle two anglers plus myself, and was comfortable and dry in open water.

Onekama Marine called in May to tell me they were now a dealer for Rampage Yachts. The Rampage Company would give me a discount on a thirty-foot Rampage in return for representing them in salmon tournaments. It would be a big investment and take time away from Florida. Dorothy and I talked it over, and as has always been the case when I had to make a major decision, we asked the Lord to pave the way.

When I returned to Onekama in June 2001, I bought the thirty-foot Rampage from Onekama Marine and sold my Tiara within the same week. I outfitted the new boat with downriggers, electronics, and rod holders to meet my requirements for salmon fishing. It was fun but time consuming to ensure everything was well thought out and did not have to be redone later.

The boat was ready by the end of July, and I was back with my salmon charters on schedule. I was sad to see the Tiara go; we had a lot of fond memories on that boat. The name on the new Rampage was—guess what—*True Blue II.*

Over the past two years, I had been thinking of expanding my business into the Bahamas, so much for cutting back. I felt there could be a market to combine a day bonefishing and a day offshore for game fish. I already had enough customers in Florida to guarantee business, so finding a location that was easily accessible with good accommodations and fishing was the first step. Since my new Rampage would be suitable for offshore fishing, I settled on Abaco, Bahamas, as the ideal location. I could keep *True Blue II* at Boat Harbor and Resort, a first-class marina located in Marsh Harbor in Abaco, Bahamas, just sixty miles and a one-hour commercial flight from Ft. Lauderdale, Florida. Abaco is known throughout the Caribbean as a tourist destination and home to several international big game fishing tournaments. It also has excellent bonefishing on the west side of the island called the Marls. I had not fished the Marls but knew people who highly recommended it.

My plan was to take my thirty-foot Rampage, *True Blue II,* to Marsh Harbor and contract with a local guide to do the bonefish trips. I would pray about it and talk to Dorothy before reaching a final decision.

The winter of 2002 went by quickly. I was busy with charters, fly casting lessons, and planning to take *True Blue II* to Florida in the fall. I did not realize how much was involved. The route would go from Onekama across Lake Michigan to Chicago and then along the inland river system to Florida. Having the right maps, learning how to transit locks, overnight stops, fuel, and marinas were just a few of the details I would have to become familiar with.

The summer salmon season was busy, partially due to several tournaments I fished representing Rampage. My agreement with Rampage required I fish three salmon tournaments using Rampage logos, pass out marketing material, and provide test rides to potential buyers. We did well in the tournaments, missing first place in one tournament by just one point. Dennis fished with us when he could but was often busy at work.

The highlight of our summer was Dennis' marriage to Donna Bajtka on September 12, 2002. Donna grew up in Manistee, a small town just south of Onekama. Her dad and mom, Gordon and Barb, still lived there. Donna and our son-in-law, Pat, have been like a daughter and son to us, loved like our own children.

# CHAPTER 16: FROM THE GREAT LAKES TO THE BAHAMAS

*"But seek first the kingdom of God and his righteousness, and all these things will be added to you." Matthew 6:33*

*Dennis Peacock Bass, Venezuela, 2001.*

I talked to Doug West, and he jumped at the chance to accompany me taking *True Blue II* to Florida and sharing the costs. Doug would be a great companion; he is both fun and a knowledgeable boater. Accompanied by my fishing buddy from Michigan, Dick Osbourne, and two friends in Dick's boat, Doug and I left Onekama for Chicago on September 27, 2002. It was rough crossing Lake Michigan; winds were out of the southwest at fifteen to twenty miles per hour with seas three to five feet. It took us eight hours to cover 160 miles to Waukegan, Illinois, where we spent the night. The next day we entered the Calumet River at Chicago, the entrance for the river system south to Florida.

The route took us along the Illinois, Ohio, Mississippi, Cumberland, Tennessee, and Tennessee-Tombigbee rivers to Mobile, Alabama, a total of 1,080 miles. I had no idea how interesting and vital the river system is to our country. Thousands of tons of cargo as well as numerous industries and towns totally depend on rivers. The history and culture of the "river people" is intriguing. We met people living on river boats that followed the sun from Minnesota to Alabama and back each year, some working along the way as needed to sustain themselves. In contrast, we met captains of expensive yachts moving boats south for the winter for their owners.

Barge traffic and locks were the biggest challenges. Stretching over 1,000 feet, barges tied together and pushed by a tug were difficult to pass. Minimum wake was the rule when passing as the tugs had little free board. We passed through seventeen locks in total; commercial boats have preference entering locks that open on a schedule. Sometimes we would go right in while other times we waited up to four hours to transit through a lock. Being squeezed between the lock wall and a tug that could crush you was unnerving at times. By the time we arrived in Mobile, we were old hands at transiting locks.

From Mobile we made our way along the intracoastal waterway to Apalachicola where we spent the night. We ate at a restaurant that only served oysters—twenty different ways! I do not remember how many dozens we ate, but it was a lot. The following morning, we left early for the 220-mile run across the Gulf of Mexico to Clearwater. We saw logger head turtles, dolphins, and various other marine creatures during the nine-hour crossing. I had high-tech navigation equipment on the boat but still relied on my compass, time, and speed just in case—a carryover from my days flying in Venezuela.

We stayed the night and refueled in Clearwater. The next day, we ran the last 100 miles from Clearwater to Gulfwind where I would keep the boat until I made the trip to the Bahamas. It took seventeen days to travel the 1,812 miles from Onekama to Gulfwind in Cape Haze. Dick Osbourne and I agreed it was a trip of a lifetime, a test of boating skills, and worth every minute. I regret I did not have more time to stop along the way. It could easily take twice as long to see everything.

I scheduled my charters to allow three weeks in December to take *True Blue II* to Marsh Harbor in the Bahamas. Doug West, who had a twenty-six-foot boat and a condo in Port St. Lucie, flew back to Florida to follow me to the Bahamas in his boat. I was delighted to have him come along for safety and the company. Doug's brother-in-law, Don, accompanied him, and my good friend and fishing buddy Chuck May made the trip with me. Chuck and I left Gulfwind on December 4 for Ft. Meyers and the Okeechobee Waterway across Florida to Port St. Lucie, 166 miles. We spent the night in Clewiston on Lake Okeechobee at Roland Martin's Fishing Resort and then continued to Port St. Lucie the follow day.

The morning of December 6, the wind was blowing hard. It is only sixty miles to Bimini, but the Gulf Stream can be rough and dangerous, so we decided to delay our crossing. We waited two days for the wind to subside. The forecast on December 9 was east ten to fifteen knots and two to four-foot waves, not ideal but safe. The first hour we made good time before entering the Gulf Stream where the waves increased to six feet with an occasional eight. Doug was having trouble keeping up, but I could not slow down as the waves would tumble over the boat; I had to stay on plane to hold my course. We lost sight of Doug for about an hour during the roughest part of the crossing. By radio, Doug said it was slow, but he and Don were still making headway.

As we moved out of the Gulf Stream into two to four-foot waves, I slowed down to wait for Doug. I tried calling but there was no answer. After a half hour, Chuck and I became concerned. I was about to turn back when we saw Doug on the horizon. Visibility was limited due to the haze, but we were sure it was him. I made radio contact, and Doug said he was so busy keeping on course he did not hear our calls. We pulled into Alice Town on Bimini wet and tired but happy to be there. The trip should have taken two and a half hours but took us four hours. It was a rough way to start our trip, no pun intended!

We cleared customs and obtained transit permits at the Compleat Angler Resort and Marina where I had reservations for two nights, giving us a day to rest and look around the island. Ernest Hemingway spent many days at the Compleat Angler during the 1930s. We were told his book *The Old Man and the Sea* was based on his experiences fishing in Bimini and Cuba. Attached to the hotel is a museum containing memorabilia of his time there. Tragically, the hotel and museum were destroyed by fire on January 13, 2006.

The next day, we crossed Grand Bahama Island through a narrow canal that bisects the island near Lucaya and headed north across the Bahama Banks to Green Turtle Cay, 160 miles north of Bimini, where we had dinner and spent the night. It was good to relax after an exciting and sometimes stressful four-day trip from Port St. Lucie. The next morning, we cruised south past Guana Cay, Man-O-War Cay, Treasure Cay, and into Marsh Harbor.

The trip from Miami to Port St. Lucie to Marsh Harbor was 300 miles; we arrived December 13, 2002. I had reserved a slip at the Boat House Marina through April. The marina had excellent facilities for transit boaters including showers and a lounge with lockers, and we stayed on our boats the entire time we were there. The next several days we explored the area; it was perfect with several good restaurants and shopping, plenty for visiting anglers to do. I contacted a bonefish guide recommended by a friend in Florida and arranged for him to take my clients for a ten percent booking fee. Chuck and I fished with the bonefish guide one day to test his skill and caught several nice bonefish.

I found a local captain at the marina to be my first mate and show me how to fish the local waters. Overall, things were coming together, and I felt we were ready to go when we flew back to Florida on December 18.

George Poveromo, host of the popular TV show *World of Saltwater* asked me to make a presentation on backcountry fly fishing for a Florida seminar in Sarasota on January 27, 2003. There were over five hundred in attendance for the one-day seminar. It was a great experience meeting George Poveromo and the other presenters, and it was gratifying for me to be included with the six other fishing experts from around Florida.

I had fifty-five trips booked in Florida for January and February. During that period, I interspersed several bookings for Marsh Harbor. The first trip was with Don Beck and three friends for two days offshore and one day bonefishing in mid-January. From the day Don arrived, the wind blew hard. Getting to the fishing grounds through Whale Harbor Channel near Marsh Harbor was a challenge when the wind blew hard from the northeast. The ocean bottom rises from 3,000 feet onto the Bahama Bank a mile from shore and creates large waves as it encounters the bank. My bonefish guide ended up with all three trips. Everything else about the trip was great: accommodations, food, transportation, and even the bonefishing.

The next two trips with different customers followed the same pattern—too windy to get offshore. We caught some nice grouper just inside the channel at Whale Harbor one day, but they had come to catch marlin and tuna. I ended up cancelling the fourth trip based on a high wind forecast. I did not have much flexibility in rescheduling customers to Marsh Harbor due to my busy schedule in Florida. The logistics and weather were proving too difficult to overcome. I did not schedule anything in Marsh Harbor after February. The plus side was Dennis came to Marsh Harbor for a week in March; we snorkeled, went bonefishing, took my boat for a sightseeing cruise of the islands, and just had a good time together.

A twinge of doubt entered my mind! Had I failed to do my homework? Was I charging ahead with *my* plans instead of God's? I was aware of the prevailing northeast winds in Florida making offshore fishing difficult during the winter months, but I had not made the connection to the Bahamas. Was I ignoring these blips on the radar screen as insignificant bumps in the road instead of the gentle nudging of the Holy Spirit to rethink my plans? Overall, things seemed to be coming together, and *True Blue II* was already in Marsh Harbor. I resolved I would wait to see how things developed. I began to ask myself, "Why am I really here?" The answer to that question would become clear over the next three months.

Doug came to visit Marsh Harbor several times, and we fished and hung out together. My brother Tom came in mid-March 2003 to help me take the boat back to Port Charlotte. Tom and I spent a couple of days in Marsh Harbor so Tom could see the area. We had a great time sightseeing and talking about the good days on the farm and our families. Doug followed us on our four-day journey from Marsh Harbor to Port St. Lucie, stopping overnight at Green Turtle Cay and the Old Bahama Bay Resort on the west end of Grand Bahama Island. We cleared customs by radio at Port St. Lucie and spent the night with Doug at his condo before heading on to Gulfwind the next day. It was the longest Tom and I had spent together since leaving high school—ten days of enjoying the scenery, the journey, and each other's company.

## PRINCIPLE 5: PATIENCE.

Patience is the capacity to accept or tolerate delay, trouble, or suffering without getting angry or upset. Waiting is all about time. It is about stopping or delaying action until the time is right to act. Lust is a psychological force producing intense desire for an object or circumstance. Lust can take many forms such as the lust for sexuality, love, money, or power, and it generally desires immediate fulfillment.

The above definitions demonstrate how impatience can morph into lust, demanding a resolution now instead of waiting for God to give the answer. A lack of patience, left unchecked, will impede our relationship with others and our trust in God. The next time you grow impatient, consider how patient God has been with you as in 2 Peter 3:9, "The Lord... is patient with you, not wanting anyone to perish, but everyone to come to repentance."

The apostle Paul was familiar with the patience of God, 1 Timothy 1:16, "But for that very reason I was shown mercy so that in me, the worst of sinners, Christ Jesus might display his immense patience as an example for those who would believe in him and receive eternal life."

Romans 8:25, "But if we hope for what we do not yet have, we wait for it patiently." We all wait at one time or another, waiting in line or for a desired outcome. It is how we wait that is important. We live in an impatient culture which must have everything now. As Christians, we might feel dejected when God does not answer our prayers on our timeline or with our expected results. God hears our prayers and always answers them in his own way and his own time. 2 Peter 3:8, "But do not forget this one thing, dear friends: With the Lord a day is like a thousand years, and a thousand years are like a day."

Patience is not something we do but rather who we are in Christ. God wants to produce patience in us to teach us to trust in him. People are not born patient. We grow in patience as we grow in Christ. It is a fruit of the Spirit and enables us to live in this demanding world and still have love, joy, and peace. My favorite verse of scripture on patience says it best: Isaiah 40:31, "but those who hope in the Lord will renew their strength. They will soar on wings like eagles; they will run and not grow weary, they will walk and not be faint."

When I got back to Riverwood, I shared my reservations with Dorothy about expanding my charter business to the Bahamas. I related to her that I had less enthusiasm for this business venture and was not sure why. Neither of us remembered talking about how fishing in the Bahamas would serve God's purpose when we had discussed expanding the business to the Bahamas a few months earlier. This is a fundamental question we have always asked before undertaking a new a new project. Every time, we have arrived at answers which we never doubted were God's will in guiding our decisions.

Looking back, we could see how subtly we had left God out of our decision. When we went to Florida, we had prayed for God to guide us. Subsequently, we were imbued with the rightness of this decision to go to Florida. This confidence, which we felt was given us from the Holy Spirit, indicated to us that we had found a new ministry and were about to make the right decision. When I planned to extend my business to the Bahamas, my main goal seemed to have been enhancing my reputation as a fisherman, and perhaps it was my ego's last attempt to confirm my expertise. I was getting older and wanted to expand my business *now*. I had become impatient and based my decision on what was best for me, ignoring the numerous obstacles God had placed in my path. Thankfully, I never lost the subtle guidance of the Holy Spirit. Unfortunately, for a short while, I was not paying attention to that guidance. With this understanding, I humbly asked the Lord to forgive me for being so impatient.

After further discussion and prayer, Dorothy and I agreed God did not want us to expand our business to the Bahamas. *True Blue II* was already back in Florida, and I would ship her back to Michigan in time for the salmon season.

It was seven a.m. April 10, 2003. I had just returned to Florida from the Bahamas with *True Blue II* a week earlier. Ed Marinaro, Jay Hodson, and I were pulling away from the dock for the first day of the Redbone Celebrity Tournament. Jay, a customer of mine from Palm Island Resort, sponsored me in the prestigious two-day tournament being held at Palm Island. All proceeds from this tournament benefit cystic fibrosis, and it was one of the most respected charity fishing tournaments in the country.

I would be guiding Jay and his friend Ed Marinaro, NFL star running back, college football hall of famer, and star of the television series *Hill Street Blues*. Other celebrities fishing in the tournament were actor James Sikking, novelist Randy White, NFL quarterback Steve Berg, NFL quarterback Earl Morrall, astronaut Bruce Melnick, and NBA center John Havlicek. During the pre-tournament dinner, Dorothy and I socialized with everyone, listening to their stories and getting to know them. Earl Morrall and I had crossed paths at Michigan State in 1953. I was on the freshman baseball team, and Earl was the starting varsity shortstop. Earl was also the star quarterback on the Michigan State football team before turning professional. We chatted about his career and family and took a few pictures. Sponsorship for the thirty-two boats in the tournament was $2,000 a boat. Points were scored based on length and species of fish. An instamatic camera and measuring board were given to each boat to record their catch. The instamatic cameras were given to judges back at the dock. Within an hour, the pictures were developed and the results posted. Our first day, we caught a couple of speckled trout and redfish but nothing to brag about; we were in the middle of the standings after the first day. On the second day, with only an hour left, Ed hooked a big fish. I knew immediately when the fish cleared the water it was a big snook and poled frantically to keep the boat away from the mangroves. Just as the fish was entering the mangroves where sharp oyster shells would have cut the fishing line, it turned away; the water was too shallow for it to go any further. Ed slowly got the upper hand and moved the fish to the boat where I gently took hold of the fish by the lower lip with my left hand and lifted it into the boat with my right hand around the tail. It was big—over thirty inches I guessed. A great shout went up from all; you would have thought we had won the Super Bowl. I took pictures of Ed and Jay and released the thirty-five-inch snook. I knew this fish could put us high on the leader board. As it happened, Ed Marinaro was the master of ceremonies at the banquet. After a delicious dinner, it was time for the presentations, and not even Ed knew the outcome. There were numerous awards for species and biggest fish. Ed won the award for biggest snook. Next came awards for best angler and best guide; Ed and I won that too. Finally, the Celebrity Grand Champion was awarded to Ed Marinaro!

I was so happy for both Ed and Jay. It was a day I will never forget. I was reflecting on the tournament afterwards and thinking of the statistical odds of having a customer I met four years earlier sponsor me in a tournament at Palm Island with Ed Marinaro who was the master of ceremonies and won the tournament with me as his guide. Not likely! I genuinely believe God had his hand in it once again.

In April, I had a commercial transporter take my Rampage back to Michigan. I did not have time to make the fifteen to seventeen-day trip by water, and it was cheaper based on fuel prices. I did not return to Onekama until June 15 to get the boat ready and start running charters.

Tournament Trail was officially formed in 2003 and had a significant impact on the growth of tournament fishing on Lake Michigan. By 2005, Tournament Trail had grown to fifteen tournaments in three states on Lake Michigan: Michigan, Indiana, and Wisconsin. The summer of 2004, I fished four Tournament Trail events, placing in the money but no wins. Rampage Yachts was working on a new thirty-three-foot sport yacht to be introduced in the spring of 2005. Jim Mrozinski asked me to accompany him to the factory in Wilmington, North Carolina, to see the boat and discuss sponsorship in the Tournament Trail. We liked what we saw; the boat was impressive trolling, at high speed, and in rough water.

I just got home from my trip to Wilmington when Donna called to let Dorothy and I know she was expecting her first child in February 2005. Dorothy and I had some soul searching to do about our future in Florida. On January 20, 2005, I would be seventy-two years old. Poling the boat everyday was beginning to take its toll physically. I had some serious skin problems and surgeries from too much sun over the years, and the housing market in Florida was spinning out of control. Would the demands of a new boat and sponsorship with Rampage Yachts be too much along with my Florida business? With news of a new granddaughter, did we really want to stay in Florida? We were beginning to see why God closed the door on the Bahamas and opened a door for us to return to Michigan.

After discussions, Rampage Yachts, Jim, and I reached an agreement on the Rampage thirty-three. I would buy the boat at a reduced price, and Rampage Yachts would sponsor me for the next five years. Jim and I would market the boat at tournaments, give test rides to potential customers, represent Rampage at boat shows, and allow the use of my name for marketing and advertising. Onekama Marine would also provide sponsorship to me where it benefitted the local market and take my thirty-foot Rampage in trade. The expected delivery of my boat would be March or April of 2005. With the details of an agreement worked out, Dorothy and I headed back to Florida.

In late October, I was giving a casting demonstration when I tore the rotator cup in my left shoulder. The surgery went well, and after six weeks of therapy, I was back to normal. The doctor questioned how long my shoulder would hold up poling a boat every day and suggested I think about giving it up. Dorothy and I did not need any more nudging from God that it was time to go back to Michigan; we wanted to be near to our grandkids as they grew up. My daughter Luanne's youngest, Grace, was now six, so it would be like starting all over again with the little ones.

Our granddaughter Carey was born on February 19, 2005, and was already two months old when we first saw her in April. What a sweetheart she was. Carey's arrival convinced us that we had made the right decision to return to Michigan.

We closed on the Rampage on May 6, 2005, and began outfitting *True Blue* for the salmon season. I considered naming the new Rampage *True Blue III,* but it sounded cumbersome to me. I had fond memories of my thirty-one foot Tiara, the original *True Blue,* and decided to honor her by using the same name. I ran my first charter on June 30. It was a busy first summer fishing six tournaments and running thirty-five charters. My tournament team consisted of my first mate, Frank, Dennis, and a couple of friends.

Before returning to Florida, Dorothy and I put a deposit on a condo at Rayner Ponds in Mason, Michigan, a few blocks from where Dennis was planning to build a new home. We decided the Onekama condo was too small for a year-round home, and with Dennis and Donna and the grandkids nearby, Mason would be a great place to live.

In September, we headed back to Florida and put our house up for sale. I told a few of my regular customers I would be leaving. Don Beck was disappointed but understood; my last trip with Don in Florida was April 11, 2005.

Houses were still selling at a rapid pace in Florida, but a slowing was evident. A few months ago, a house would sell within days; now it was a few weeks. We listed the house with a broker at a sizeable increase over what we paid for it. By Christmas 2005 we had several inquiries but no offers. In January 2006, Dorothy met a couple at the golf club who came to see our house that afternoon. After their offer and our counteroffer, we agreed on a price including the golf membership and golf cart and closed in early February with an option to rent until our departure in April. We arranged for Palmer Moving and Storage to pack and move our belongings to storage in Dearborn, Michigan, until our condo in Rayner Ponds was ready.

We got out just in time; by summer there were sixty homes for sale in Riverwood and the market was in free fall. Dorothy was busy getting us ready to move again. She was an expert at overseeing the packing and selling items we did not take with us. I sold my Hell's Bay in March—a sad day for me. I called Rayner Ponds to confirm our new condo would be ready by July 2006. We arrived in Onekama by mid-April after a stop in Mason to visit with our new granddaughter and her mom and dad. Driving home from Florida, Dorothy and I looked back on the almost fourteen years in Florida. What a wonderful "assignment" it had been. Just like our relocations around the world with Ford, we were leaving fond memories and friends behind. This assignment had been a little longer than normal and was perhaps our last relocation, but we said that the last time. We were excited to learn what the Lord had in store for us next.

In February 2006, Jim Mrozinski and I went to the Miami Boat Show to launch Rampage Yachts on the Great Lakes. There were large three by four-foot color posters of me and my Rampage and advertisements in major boating and fishing magazines. Tred Barta, host of the popular NBC television program *The Best and Worst of Tred Barta* would be using the Rampage thirty-three on his TV program.

It was an unforgettable season that started with an improbable win. The first tournament of the season, aptly named the Onekama Marine Shake Down, was on Memorial Day weekend. To compete, you weigh in your five biggest fish each day. We fished the barrel, one of my favorite fishing spots but didn't catch anything. After the first day, we were in last place, sixty pounds behind the leader. There was a little snickering and others who were surprised that *True Blue* "got skunked," a dreaded word to any charter captain.

At the six-a.m. shot gun start from the Onekama pierhead the next morning, I started to follow many boats running south to Manistee, but after a few minutes I made a sudden 180-degree turn and headed north toward the barrel. Chuck, Gary, and Frank looked at me in surprise, "I thought we were going to fish the shelf by Manistee," Chuck said, "that's where all the fish were caught yesterday."

"I know," I said, "but we know there are fish in the barrel, we just couldn't get them to bite. I have a feeling they will bite today!" The crew was skeptical, but I was the captain, so we headed for the barrel. Back at the weigh-in, there was much excitement and anticipation as participants waited for the fish to be weighed. When we put our fish on the scale, there were shouts of glee and groans of despair. Some could not believe it—how could we have such a big catch in the barrel today and get skunked the day before? We ended up in second place in the Onekama Marine Shake Down, won the 333 Championship Series event, and won the biggest fish of the tournament. That win in the 333 Championship Series, followed by a win at the Budweiser Pro-Am tournament in Manistee two weeks later, started us on our way to a great season, placing second in the overall 333 Championship Series and winning the season-long, winner take all, side bet at Bay Harbor in September.

# CHAPTER 17: RETURN TO MICHIGAN

*"There is a time for everything, and a season for every activity under the heavens."*
*Ecclesiastes 3:1*

*Rampage 33, 2006.*

We moved into our condo at Rayner Ponds on July 26, 2006. We were twenty minutes from my old alma mater, Michigan State University, and four hours from Pat and Luanne in Lebanon, Ohio, and to our condo in Onekama. Dorothy and I had not realized the benefit of living near a university. There are unlimited activities to suit the young and old. Sports activities, broadways plays, medical facilities, continuing education programs, and just walking on the beautiful campus.

In July, we put our dog Daisy to sleep; she was twelve years old and could no longer get around on her own. In September, we picked up an eight-week-old yellow female Labrador from a breeder in Goshen, Indiana. We decided to name her Daisy as a tribute to our last Daisy. The next several years were busy with family, charters, training Daisy, and community projects. I was elected to the board of the Manistee County Sport Fishing Association, the Portage Lake Harbor Commission, and the Michigan Port Collaborative. All these organizations are involved with fishery conservation and enhancing our water resources.

On June 19, 2007, our granddaughter, Amanda, was born. We were so happy for Dennis and Donna and even happier that we lived so close. We had been visiting local churches and liked the Mason First Church of the Nazarene where we have been attending ever since. We got to know the pastor, Gerhard Weigelt, in a personal way when Dennis was diagnosed with a tumor on his adrenal gland and underwent surgery at the University of Michigan Hospital in Ann Arbor in March 2013. Part of the adrenal gland was successfully removed, and Dennis made a complete recovery, thank the Lord. Pastor Gerhart spent the day with us at the hospital during the surgery, and we felt blessed to have him there.

During the winters of 2007 to 2010, we had fun snowmobiling and skiing. This was a big change from the prior fourteen winters in Florida. Dorothy and I missed Florida, but with the grandkids so close and many activities to do, we were glad to be back in Michigan. I also admit to feeling older; I was now in my mid-seventies and slowing down a bit. Not having to be on the water every day made life a lot easier. My granddaughter Emilee, now a student at Michigan State University, was only twenty minutes from our condo in Mason. Emilee came over for a home-cooked meal or to spend the night every chance she had!

During the summers of 2007 to 2010, the tournament schedule and representing Rampage reduced my charters to about forty per summer. Coupled with fishing eight tournaments, it was all I could handle. In addition, I assisted Onekama Marine at boat shows. My role was to represent the Rampage line with onboard presentations and demos to potential buyers.

The highlight of the 2010 season was Tight Lines for Troops. Captain Bob Guenthhardt, a former Ogema—chief—of the Little River Band and Army veteran, conceived the idea in the fall of 2009. With the help of the Little River Casino in Manistee and a host of volunteers, the first charity salmon fishing tournament for Michigan Veterans took place May 15, 2010, with sixty charter boats and over two hundred and fifty veterans participating. It was an honor to host these deserving veterans, some from World War II. The popular tournament continues to this day.

By 2010, the downturn in the US economy was negatively impacting boat manufacturers and participation in tournaments. Rampage Yachts cut back on production and ended my sponsorship agreement the spring of 2010. We all benefited from our five years together: Onekama Marine sold eight Rampages, a new Rampage dealer was added on Lake Erie in 2006, and I had five years of financial support and a beautiful boat that I owned. Most importantly, I had five years of unforgettable memories fishing with family and friends at ports all over Lake Michigan—something I would not have been able to do on my own.

On November 18, 2010, Dennis Michael Blue was born. He is the fifth generation of the Blue family to be named Dennis. I was so proud to have a grandson to carry on the name. No matter the name, I love them all.

Tom and Joann were blessed with six children: Tommy, Michael, David, Danny, Mary Ann, and Kathy. All went to high school or college, married, have successful careers, and settled close to Tom and Joann in Frederick, Maryland. David, the third oldest and 6'7" moved to Pittsburg. He was a star basketball player in high school and played with Patrick Ewing at Georgetown University.

In 2010, there were difficult times for the Blue family. In early 2010 Kathy (Blue) Shores, the youngest, was diagnosed with

Multiple Sclerosis. As her condition worsened, she had to give up her career as a dental hygienist and is now confined to a wheelchair. Her husband, Dave, and two young children, Olivia and Christopher, have shown remarkable support and love caring for her. We continue to pray for her healing and trust God for the future.

On July 19, 2010, Dorothy and I got a call from Tom that their oldest son, Tommy, had been killed in a car accident. We were devastated. Tommy was fifty-two years old, divorced, and had four grown daughters. He had just retired two years earlier. Tommy was one of a kind—a big man with a big beard who loved the outdoors. He was born one hundred years too late; a mountain man would best describe him.

On June 11, 2011, Dennis took me on another fishing trip to Alaska. His job was going well, and he wanted to try a different lodge that combined salmon and halibut fishing. We flew from Detroit to Anchorage, where we stayed the night, and the next day took a local flight to the Deep Creek Fishing Lodge on the Kenai Peninsula. It was first class all the way: accommodations, guides, and equipment. We fished three days for salmon and halibut, shipping home 60 pounds of frozen fillets.

The biggest halibut was 145 pounds, caught by Dennis of course. The highlight of the trip, however, was not the fishing. Each night we gathered for dinner around a large round table that seated fourteen including the owner of the lodge, his wife, and twelve guests to chat about the day's fishing. One evening, we learned one of the guests, John, had arrhythmia, an irregular heartbeat, and his medication was not helping.

The next night at dinner, I asked how he was feeling. John said not good; he was still having a problem with his heartbeat and if it did not improve by morning, he would seek medical help in Anchorage. There was obvious concern from others at the table, and the owner said he would check in with him later that night. I made eye contact with John and said we would pray for his healing. He smiled and said thank you while others nodded or just looked on. When we got back to the room that night, Dennis and I prayed for John, not only to heal the gentleman but to provide a witness for the others.

We did not see John the next morning and wondered how he was doing. No one was sure but thought he went fishing. That night at dinner, John looked better. After we all were seated, John wanted to make an announcement. He looked at Dennis and me and said, "Thank you for your prayers. I went back to my room last night to rest, and about two a.m. I awoke and my heartbeat was normal." Everyone lifted their glasses in celebration. I said, "Do not thank me, thank the Lord," and a few others said amen.

In January 2013, we lost my brother Tom. He had been suffering from respiratory problems for a few years and was on medication. Joann called just after Christmas to tell us he had been admitted to the hospital due to breathing problems but seemed to be doing better. We were concerned but cautiously optimistic. The next day, Tom called me from the hospital to say he was doing fine and expected to be released in a day or two. He sounded weak but seemed in good spirits. After we hung up, I had an uneasy feeling, something telling me all was not well. The timing and tone of our conversation sounded like Tom called to say goodbye. Two days later we heard Tom was in intensive care. They would let us know of any changes or if we should come to Frederick. Tom passed away the next day—January 7, 2013—at age seventy-eight. Tom was buried in Frederick next to his son Tommy. All the Tom Blue and Dennis Blue families were there to bid farewell to Tom; he will be missed.

During the 2013 season, I realized it was time to give up chartering. I was eighty years old and slowing down. My first mate, Frank, had been performing most of the physically demanding activities during the past several years. I was the captain, but Frank did the heavy work of fishing. Each year, the number of charters diminished, just enough to keep pace with my physical ability. I had never thought of it quite this way before, but my charter business was slowly dying off. Literally, many of my original customers had passed away or were no longer physically able to go fishing.

Frank had a good job at Dunham's Sporting Goods, and I was not booking enough charters to keep a first mate busy. I put the boat up for sale in January 2014. I placed an advertisement in the 2015 Tournament Trail magazine and sold my Rampage on May 5, 2015. Thank you, Lord.

I had mixed emotions about selling *True Blue*. I knew the time had come; I could no longer physically perform the duties of a charter captain, and the cost of owning the boat without the charter income was prohibitive. From a financial point of view, it was the right decision. Accepting the fact that another chapter in my life had ended was not as easy. I missed seeing my fishing buddies and most of all the ministry of witnessing to others on my boat. There would be no change of career as was the case when I left Ford.

# CHAPTER 18: LIFE AFTER FISHING

*"The Lord bless you and keep you;*
*the Lord make his face shine on you and be*
*gracious to you; the Lord turn his face toward*
*you and give you peace." Numbers 6:24-26*

*(left to right) Dennis, Dennis, John, George, and*
*Chris. Bud-Pro Am winners, Manistee, 2006.*

I miss the charter business now and then but keep busy with things that are not as strenuous. I have more free time with the grandkids, walking my lab Daisy, and other projects such as writing. Dorothy, on the other hand, asks me frequently, "Don't you think it's time for you to go fishing again?" In my Ford career, God used Ford as the vehicle to move Dorothy and me around the world to serve his purpose. In my second career God has used my charter boat *True Blue* as the vehicle to serve his purpose witnessing to people from all walks of life. God strategically places each of us to serve him.

In 2017, I was surprised and humbled to receive the Unprecedented Commitment to the Manistee County Sport Fishing Association Award. Formed in the 1980s, MCSFA advocates for and promotes fishing and conservation in Manistee County. I have been a member since its inception, serving in various capacities and on the board.

Dorothy and I try to stay out of the details of being parents again. Occasionally, we venture an opinion, but for the most part we let the parents be parents and grandparents be grandparents. What we notice most is that things that seemed so important at the time we were raising our own children really were not that important after all. Like most parents, we made our share of mistakes, but our kids did not turn out that bad. On a more serious note, we are so proud of our sons and daughters, which of course includes their spouses and families. Watching the children and grandchildren grow up reminded me of how things change. Cultures, music, and lifestyles all impact how future generations view the world. There is one constant however and that is the infallible Word of God, the same yesterday, today, and forever. The greatest legacy Dorothy and I will leave behind are not fame nor fortune but families that love the Lord.

With Luanne's encouragement, I wrote and self-published two books in 2018—*Running the Good Race* and *Through the Eyes of a Fisherman*—autobiographies about my life with Ford and as a charter captain. It was great fun filtering through old photos and reliving those years. We are so blessed.

In October 2018, Dorothy was diagnosed with Alzheimer's. The disease has slowly robbed her of many memories she held dear to her heart. I miss her vibrant personality and positive attitude. I miss our discussions about Jesus and how God directed us to serve his purpose. Being a caretaker can bring out the best and the worst in you. Initially, I resisted and perhaps resented her change in behavior. I did not realize the effort and responsibility of a caregiver. Then, God helped me see his plan: as I drew closer to Dorothy and to God, I gained more patience, and I learned love is most meaningful when you receive nothing in return.

In the fall of 2020, I started writing again. Using life experiences from my previous autobiographies, I focused on the five biblical principles that have guided me throughout my life: prayer, purpose, perspective, passion, and patience. It was only after I completed my second book, *Through the Eyes of a Fisherman*, that I began to conceptualize these principles and put them into words. Jesus has been with me all my Christian life, providing his guidance through the Holy Spirit. I began to see how my decisions and actions had been influenced by these principles as I applied them to my life.

"Be strong and courageous. Do not be afraid or terrified because of them, for the Lord your God goes with you; he will never leave you nor forsake you." Deuteronomy 31:6. Remember God is always there. The wisdom of these biblical principles never changes; the application of the principles to your life depends on your daily walk with him through the Holy Spirit. I pray they will be as enlightening to you as they were for me.

Unexpectedly, I had a detached retina in my left eye a month after I started this book. It took three surgeries to reattach the retina and another six months to regain some eyesight. Thank the Lord for good vision in my right eye. My book writing came to a halt during the recuperation and did not resume until January 2021. I may have rushed the editing and publishing timetable a bit, but at age eighty-eight, time is of the essence!

As you grow older, your perspective of life grows larger. You focus less on day to day and more on eternity. Faith becomes reality because you have lived it—things hoped for and seen. The mirror of life is still hazy but grows clearer each day. God's perspective grows and our earthly perspective diminishes.

As important as they are, I try not to focus on past memories but let the word of God continue to grow and be active in my daily life. Growing old physically is not growing old spiritually. The cheers of the saints in heaven grows louder as you near the finish line. I am not finished yet; I may have another book to write.

If you do not already know Jesus, I encourage you to ask him into your life; you will not regret it.

# ACKNOWLEDGEMENTS

Thank you to my family who encouraged me to keep on writing and share how God has blessed our lives.

A special thanks to Julie Taylor who provided the editing, lay out, design, and publishing skills. Her insight and Christian perspective made it possible to integrate real life experiences with the biblical principles that guided my life.

Finally, to the numerous friends who provided advice, corrective comments, and advance reader copy book reviews, thank you for your support.

# NOTE TO MY READERS

To my readers, thank you for reading *Need Direction? Ask God*. I pray that God will use this story to empower your life with his infinite wisdom and bring glory to his name.

One of the most important things an author can do for their book is to obtain Amazon customer reviews, and I would appreciate your help with this. Go to www.amazon.com/books, type the title of my book in the search bar at the top of the page, click on *Need Direction? Ask God,* and scroll down to Customer Reviews/Review this Product to leave your review. If you have questions or need additional information, go to my website www.trueblueauthor.com.